MISS GRAND INTERNATIONAL

Hey there, Adventurous Artist!

Welcome to the dazzling world of "Kaleidoscope of Cultures"! Your hands are holding way more than just a coloring book; it's a ticket to a global adventure, where every page is a new country to explore and every color you choose tells a unique story.

Imagine visiting countries across our amazing planet, meeting people from different cultures, and exploring their incredible traditions and stories, all through your coloring journey. Each page brings you designs from the Miss Grand International Pageant's National Costume Competition (2021), where costumes tell stories about their countries' myths, landscapes, history, and even yummy foods!

Now, it's your turn to splash your favorite colors on these costumes, bringing them to life in your own vibrant style. Imagine the fun stories, the secret tales, and the awesome adventures each outfit has witnessed! Whether you dream up bold, exciting colors or choose to explore with soft, gentle shades, every page is YOUR adventure to create.

As you dive into this coloring quest, remember that every color you lay down connects you to people and places from around the world, celebrating the super cool tapestry of our global family.

Enjoy every moment, create epic adventures, and let's celebrate the beautiful diversity of our world together through your art!

Happy Coloring!

All Right Reserved © Miss Grand International Public Company Limited

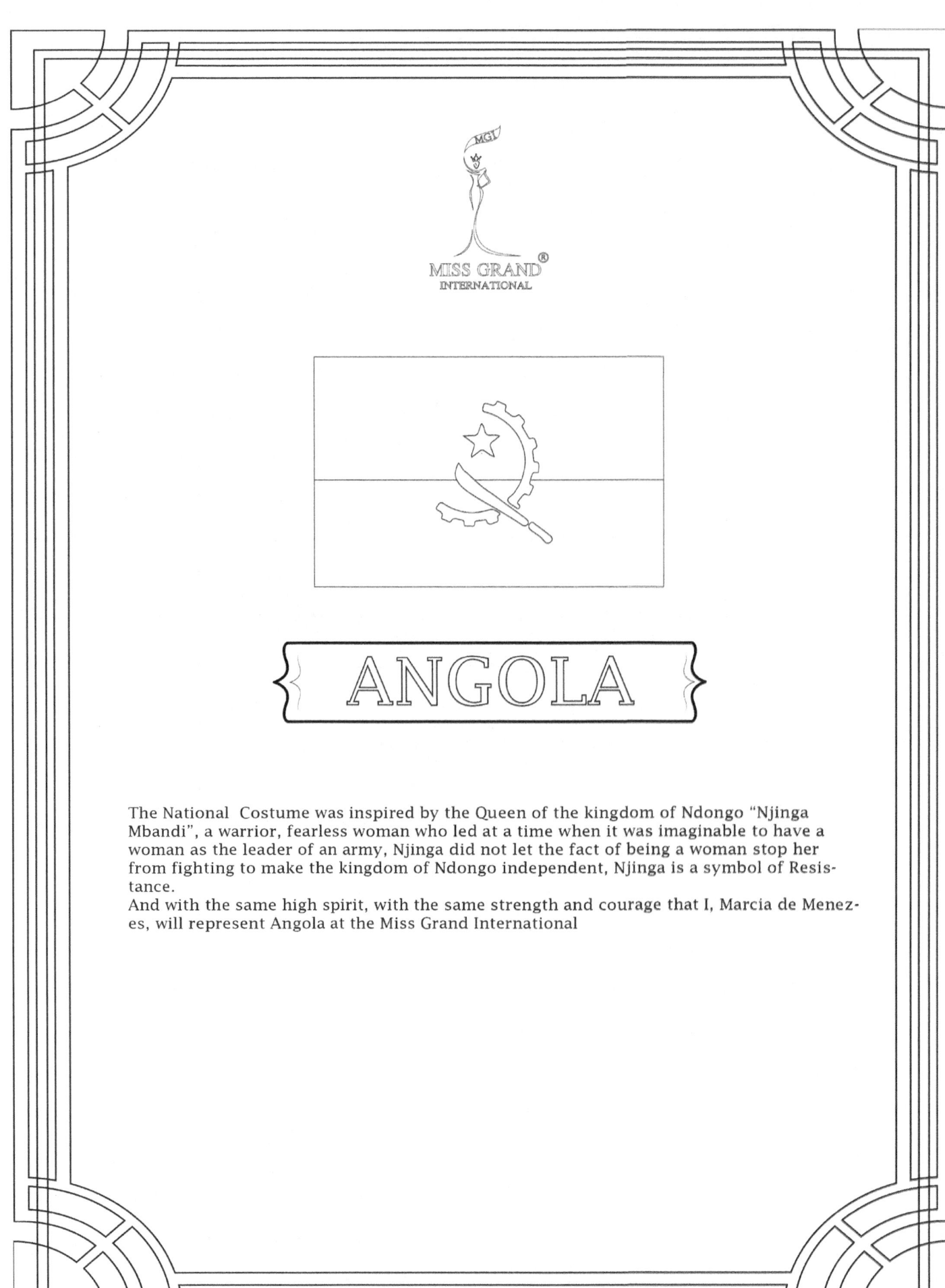

{ ANGOLA }

The National Costume was inspired by the Queen of the kingdom of Ndongo "Njinga Mbandi", a warrior, fearless woman who led at a time when it was imaginable to have a woman as the leader of an army, Njinga did not let the fact of being a woman stop her from fighting to make the kingdom of Ndongo independent, Njinga is a symbol of Resistance.
And with the same high spirit, with the same strength and courage that I, Marcia de Menezes, will represent Angola at the Miss Grand International

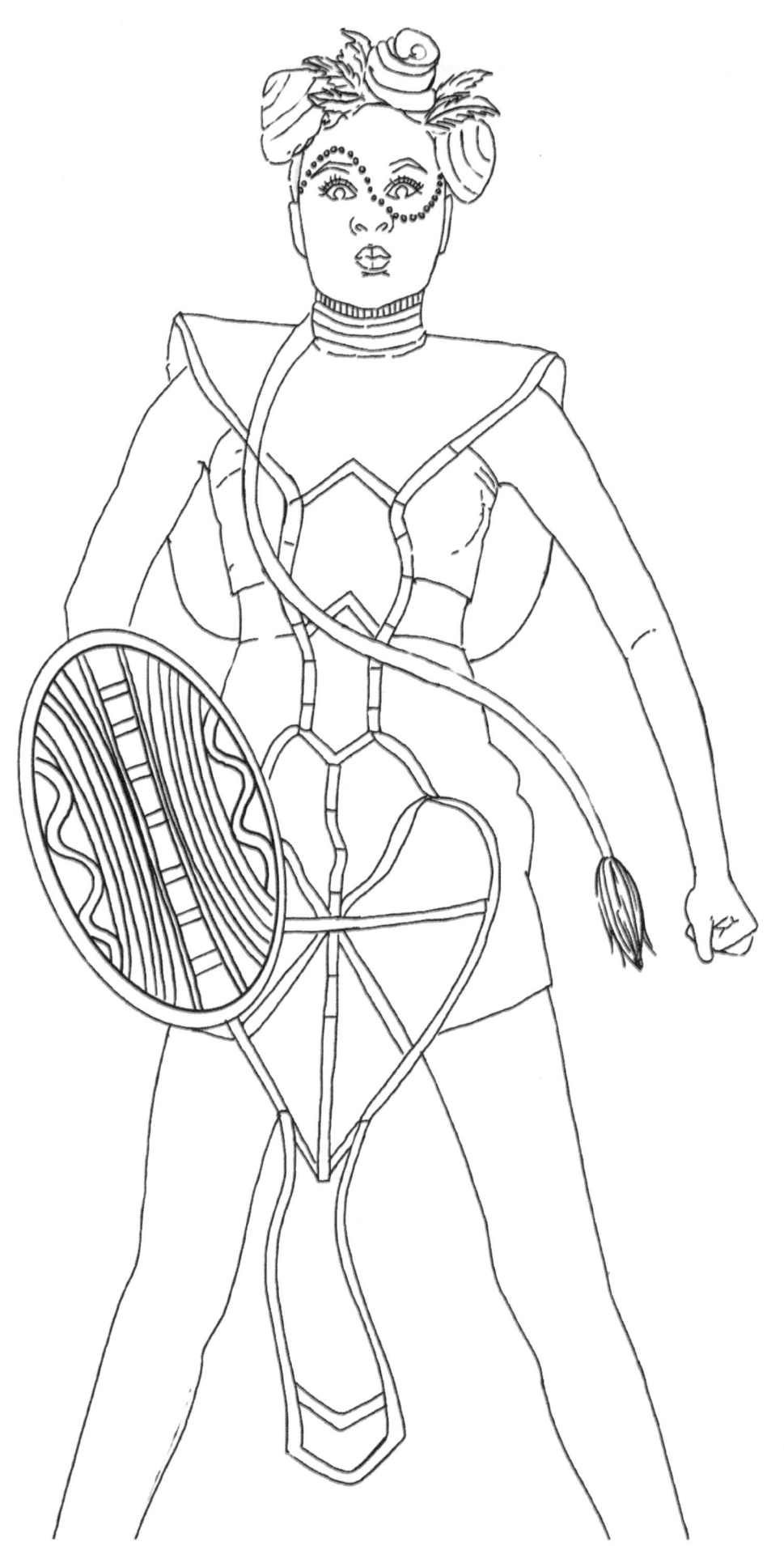

{ARGENTINA}

In this opportunity Miss Grand International Argentina represents the tulip fields located in "Trevelin", a town of Chubut near The Andes mountain range. These fields stand out for their wonderful and colorful contrast with the rest of the natural landscape full of rocky mountains.

This characteristic garment has been made with: rock crystals, mirrored crystal rhinestones and opal, crimped oval cut crystals and rivoli cut stones enhanced with crystal rhinestones, un-crimped flat crystals, Hot Fix and metallic filigree beads; Strips of pasamanería (textile craftwork trimming, involving intertwined cords) and Lurex ribbons. All these to evoke the shiny refractions of light made by the sunrise when it touches the dew drops that bathe the tulip fields every morning during springtime and make them appear almost crystal made.

Framing and complementing Florencia's figure, there are:
- Two duck feather fans in the range of color that goes from a hot pink to a pastel one.
- Tow cascading side wings made of 30 to 45 cm white rooster feathers.

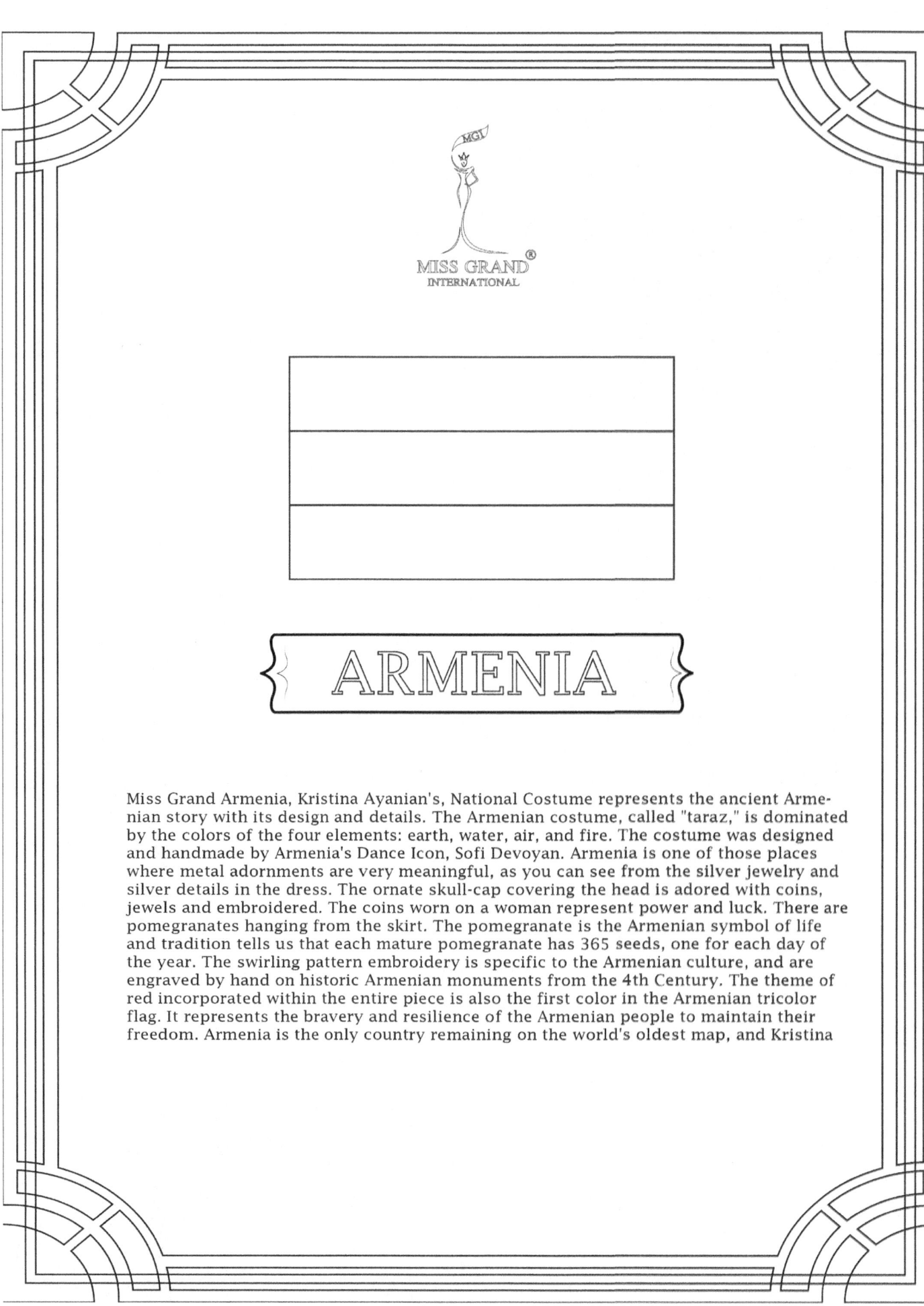

{ ARMENIA }

Miss Grand Armenia, Kristina Ayanian's, National Costume represents the ancient Armenian story with its design and details. The Armenian costume, called "taraz," is dominated by the colors of the four elements: earth, water, air, and fire. The costume was designed and handmade by Armenia's Dance Icon, Sofi Devoyan. Armenia is one of those places where metal adornments are very meaningful, as you can see from the silver jewelry and silver details in the dress. The ornate skull-cap covering the head is adored with coins, jewels and embroidered. The coins worn on a woman represent power and luck. There are pomegranates hanging from the skirt. The pomegranate is the Armenian symbol of life and tradition tells us that each mature pomegranate has 365 seeds, one for each day of the year. The swirling pattern embroidery is specific to the Armenian culture, and are engraved by hand on historic Armenian monuments from the 4th Century. The theme of red incorporated within the entire piece is also the first color in the Armenian tricolor flag. It represents the bravery and resilience of the Armenian people to maintain their freedom. Armenia is the only country remaining on the world's oldest map, and Kristina

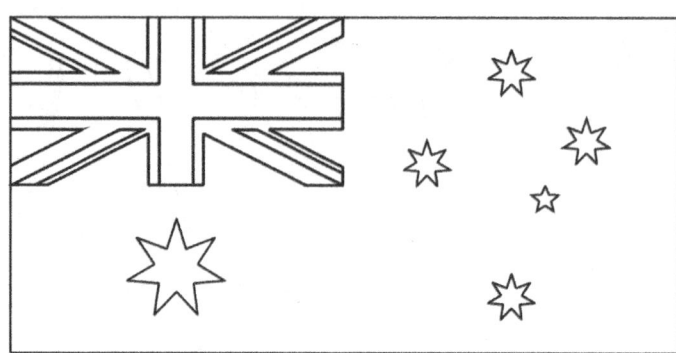

AUSTRALIA

Ulysses butterfly is a large swallowtail butterfly of Australia. It is a brilliant electric blue colour with a wingspan of about 10.5cm. This butterfly is used as an emblem for tourism in Queensland, Australia, the home of the Great Barrier Reef & the daintree rainforest, the world's oldest tropical rainforest!

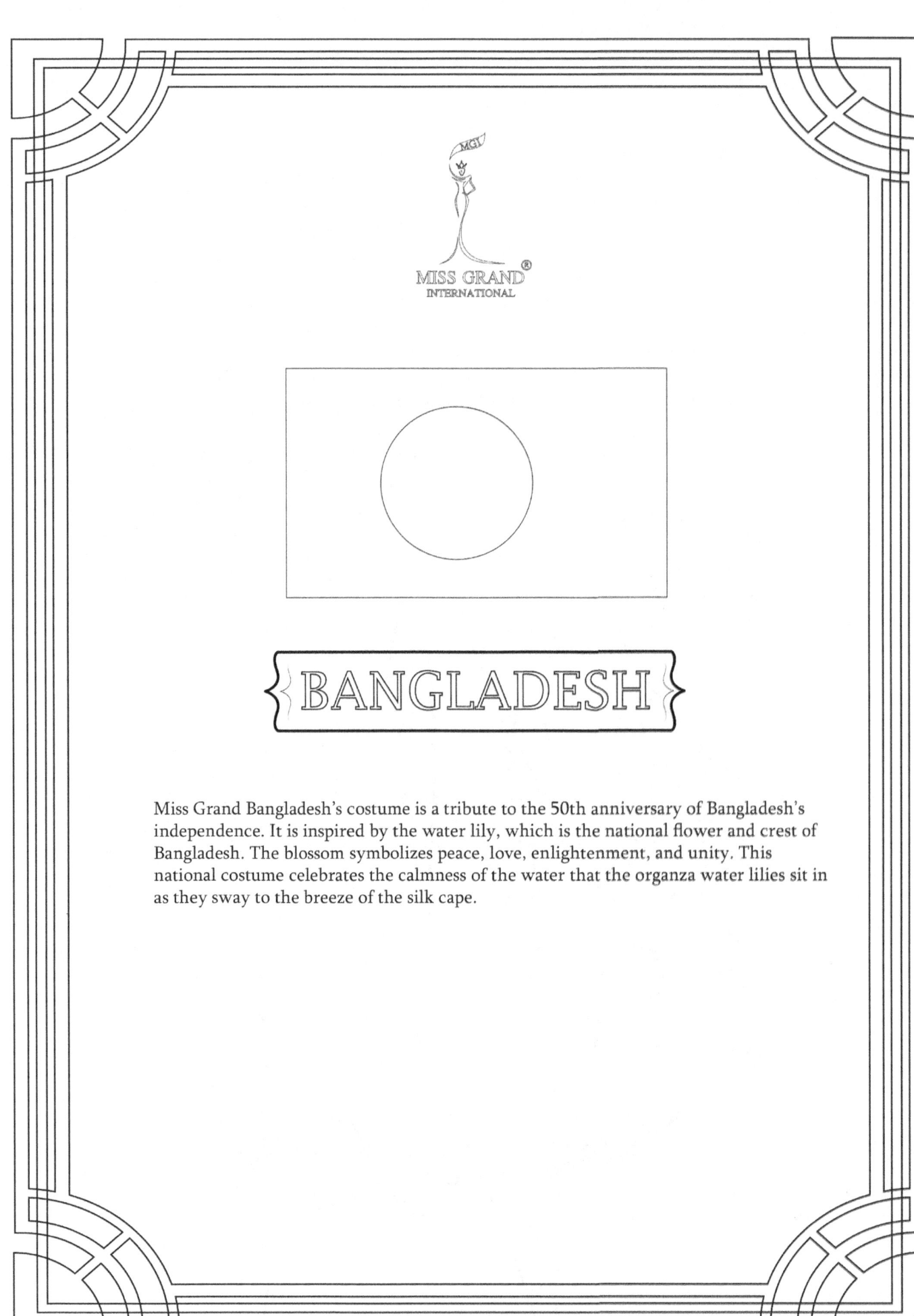

BANGLADESH

Miss Grand Bangladesh's costume is a tribute to the 50th anniversary of Bangladesh's independence. It is inspired by the water lily, which is the national flower and crest of Bangladesh. The blossom symbolizes peace, love, enlightenment, and unity. This national costume celebrates the calmness of the water that the organza water lilies sit in as they sway to the breeze of the silk cape.

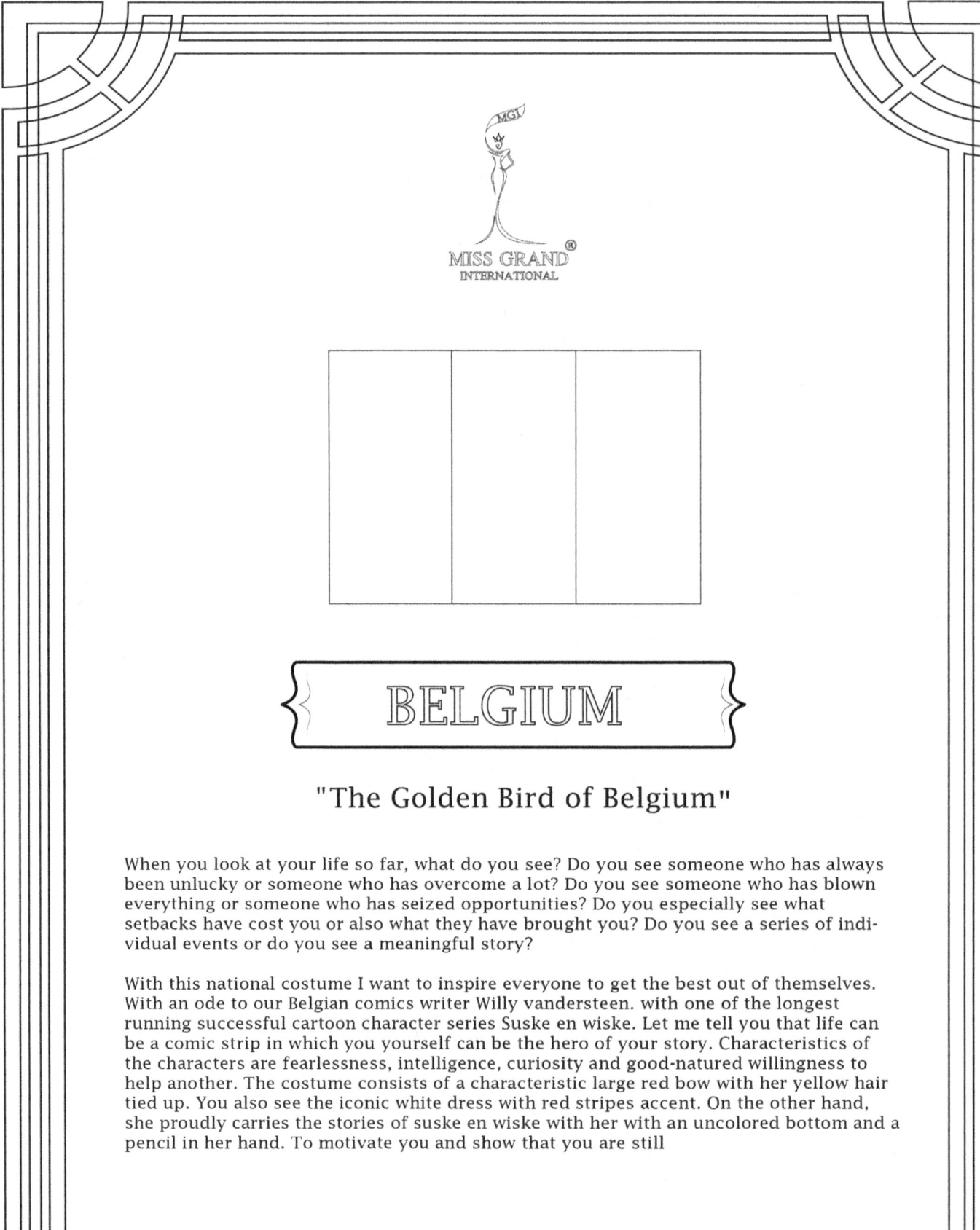

BELGIUM

"The Golden Bird of Belgium"

When you look at your life so far, what do you see? Do you see someone who has always been unlucky or someone who has overcome a lot? Do you see someone who has blown everything or someone who has seized opportunities? Do you especially see what setbacks have cost you or also what they have brought you? Do you see a series of individual events or do you see a meaningful story?

With this national costume I want to inspire everyone to get the best out of themselves. With an ode to our Belgian comics writer Willy vandersteen. with one of the longest running successful cartoon character series Suske en wiske. Let me tell you that life can be a comic strip in which you yourself can be the hero of your story. Characteristics of the characters are fearlessness, intelligence, curiosity and good-natured willingness to help another. The costume consists of a characteristic large red bow with her yellow hair tied up. You also see the iconic white dress with red stripes accent. On the other hand, she proudly carries the stories of suske en wiske with her with an uncolored bottom and a pencil in her hand. To motivate you and show that you are still

BOLIVIA

The elaboration of this typical costume is based on the recycling of some synthetic materials. The headdress is handcrafted of papier-mâché, lined with synthetic leather. In the center is represented the "Lord of the Staves" that mystical being that represents the Sun and is located on the monolith that is called "La Puerta del Sol" which describes the position of the sun at any time or time of day. The pheasant feathers that represent the splendor of this culture are collected one by one from the molting that these birds make each year.

Numerous turquoise, quartz and wood beads were used in the bustier. The cauda shows fossil remains of ammonites, hand painted in oil. A tail cap is detached from the waist that contains the representation of "Estela or Monolito Pachamama" considered a world heritage site since 2002..

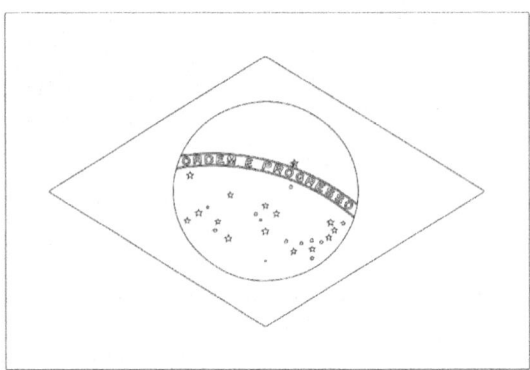

{ BRAZIL }

Boitatá, protector of the forests, is a character in Brazilian folklore.

The legend of Boitatá describes this mythic character as a great snake of fire. It protects animals and forests from people who do them harm and, above all, who carry out fires in the forests.

In the folkloric narrative, this snake can transform itself into a burning log with the intention of deceiving and burning the invaders and destroyers of the forests. It is believed that the person who looks at Boitatá becomes blind and crazy!

The base of the costume is made of hand-painted mesh, embroidered with small inserts all over the body to give the illusion of scales. There are also micro crystals in gradient, and digital LED to give the effect of burning flames. To the public's surprise, a small mechanism will be used to make the miss's "tiara" turn into the head of a snake!

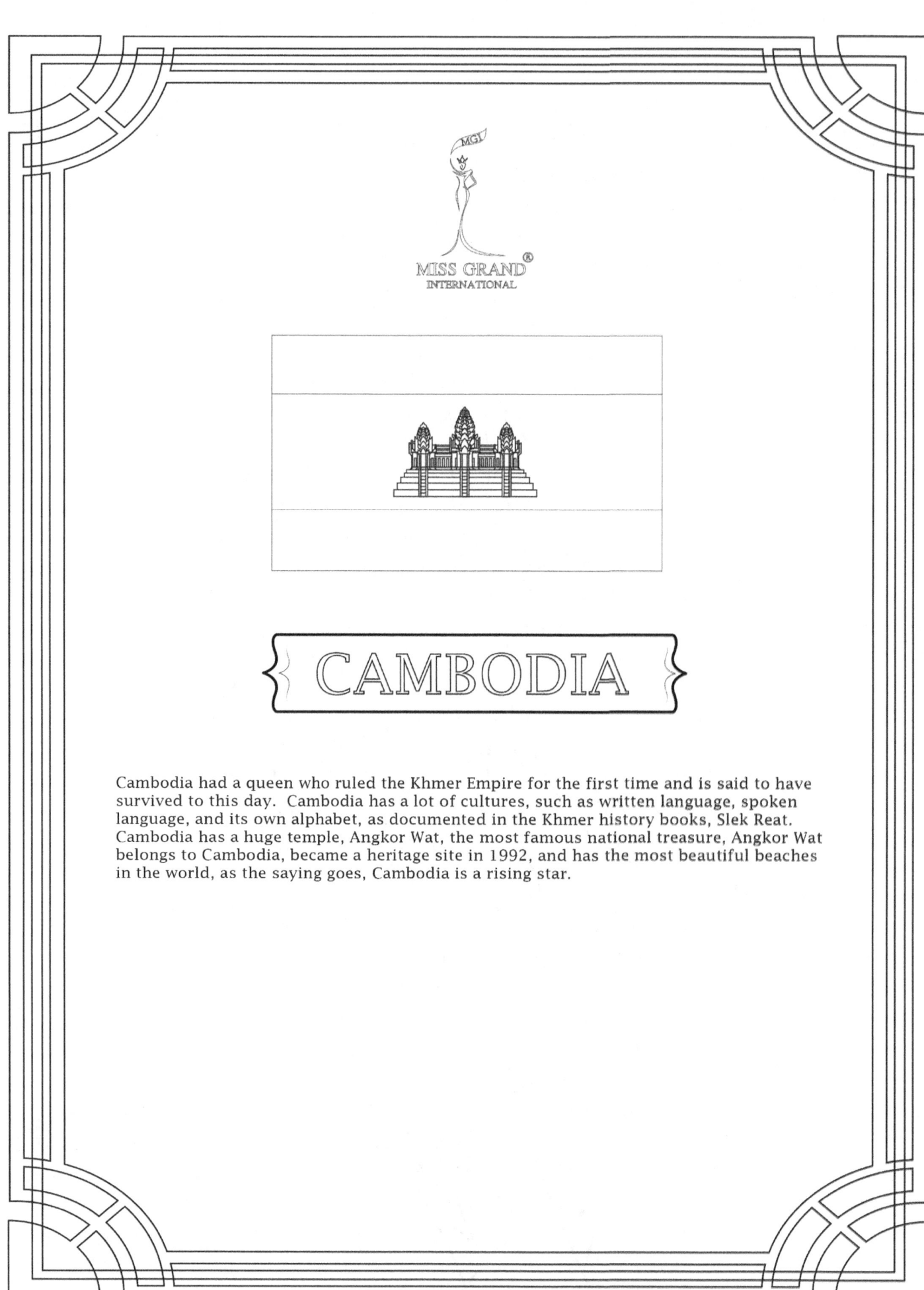

CAMBODIA

Cambodia had a queen who ruled the Khmer Empire for the first time and is said to have survived to this day. Cambodia has a lot of cultures, such as written language, spoken language, and its own alphabet, as documented in the Khmer history books, Slek Reat. Cambodia has a huge temple, Angkor Wat, the most famous national treasure, Angkor Wat belongs to Cambodia, became a heritage site in 1992, and has the most beautiful beaches in the world, as the saying goes, Cambodia is a rising star.

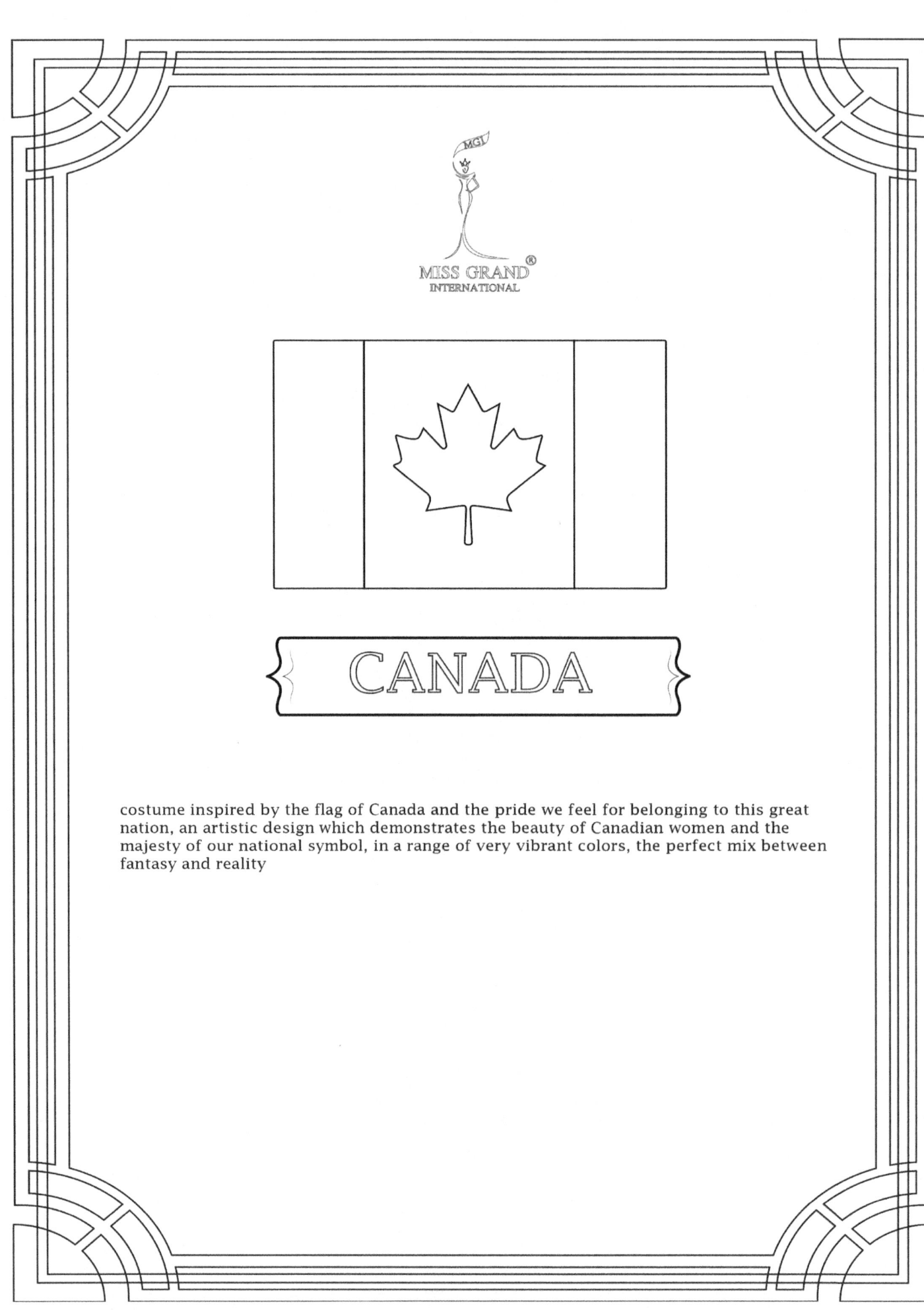

costume inspired by the flag of Canada and the pride we feel for belonging to this great nation, an artistic design which demonstrates the beauty of Canadian women and the majesty of our national symbol, in a range of very vibrant colors, the perfect mix between fantasy and reality

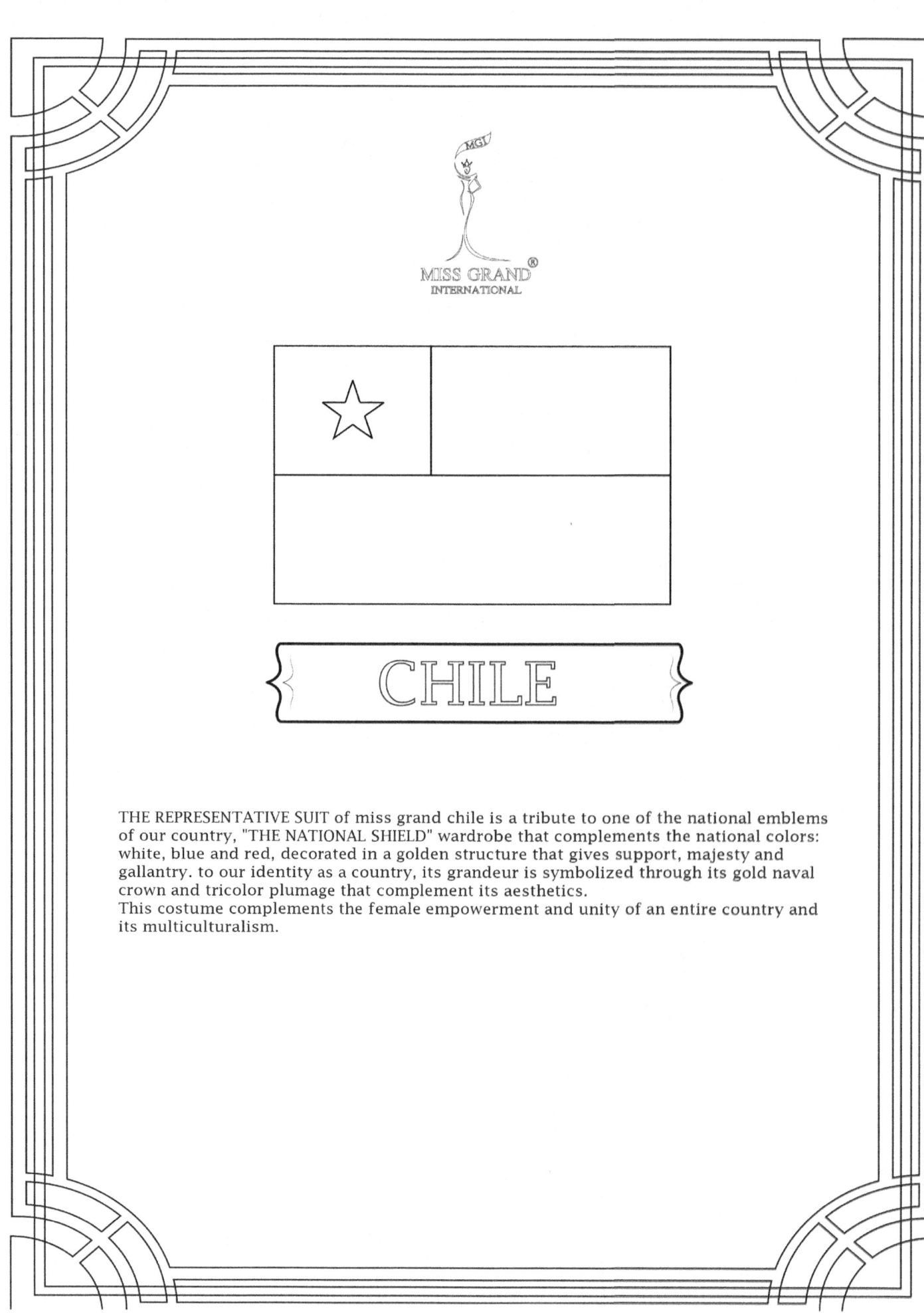

CHILE

THE REPRESENTATIVE SUIT of miss grand chile is a tribute to one of the national emblems of our country, "THE NATIONAL SHIELD" wardrobe that complements the national colors: white, blue and red, decorated in a golden structure that gives support, majesty and gallantry. to our identity as a country, its grandeur is symbolized through its gold naval crown and tricolor plumage that complement its aesthetics.
This costume complements the female empowerment and unity of an entire country and its multiculturalism.

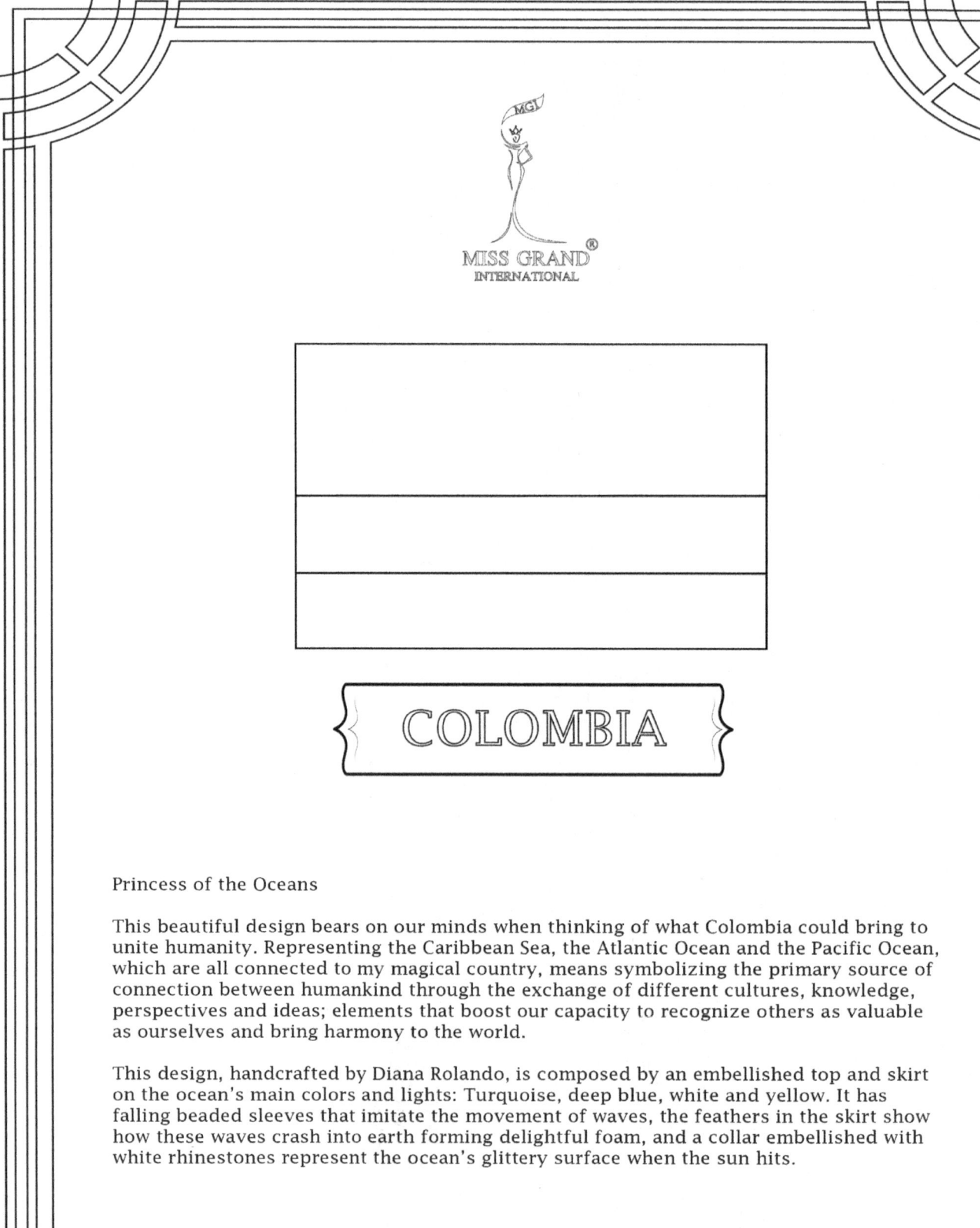

{ COLOMBIA }

Princess of the Oceans

This beautiful design bears on our minds when thinking of what Colombia could bring to unite humanity. Representing the Caribbean Sea, the Atlantic Ocean and the Pacific Ocean, which are all connected to my magical country, means symbolizing the primary source of connection between humankind through the exchange of different cultures, knowledge, perspectives and ideas; elements that boost our capacity to recognize others as valuable as ourselves and bring harmony to the world.

This design, handcrafted by Diana Rolando, is composed by an embellished top and skirt on the ocean's main colors and lights: Turquoise, deep blue, white and yellow. It has falling beaded sleeves that imitate the movement of waves, the feathers in the skirt show how these waves crash into earth forming delightful foam, and a collar embellished with white rhinestones represent the ocean's glittery surface when the sun hits.

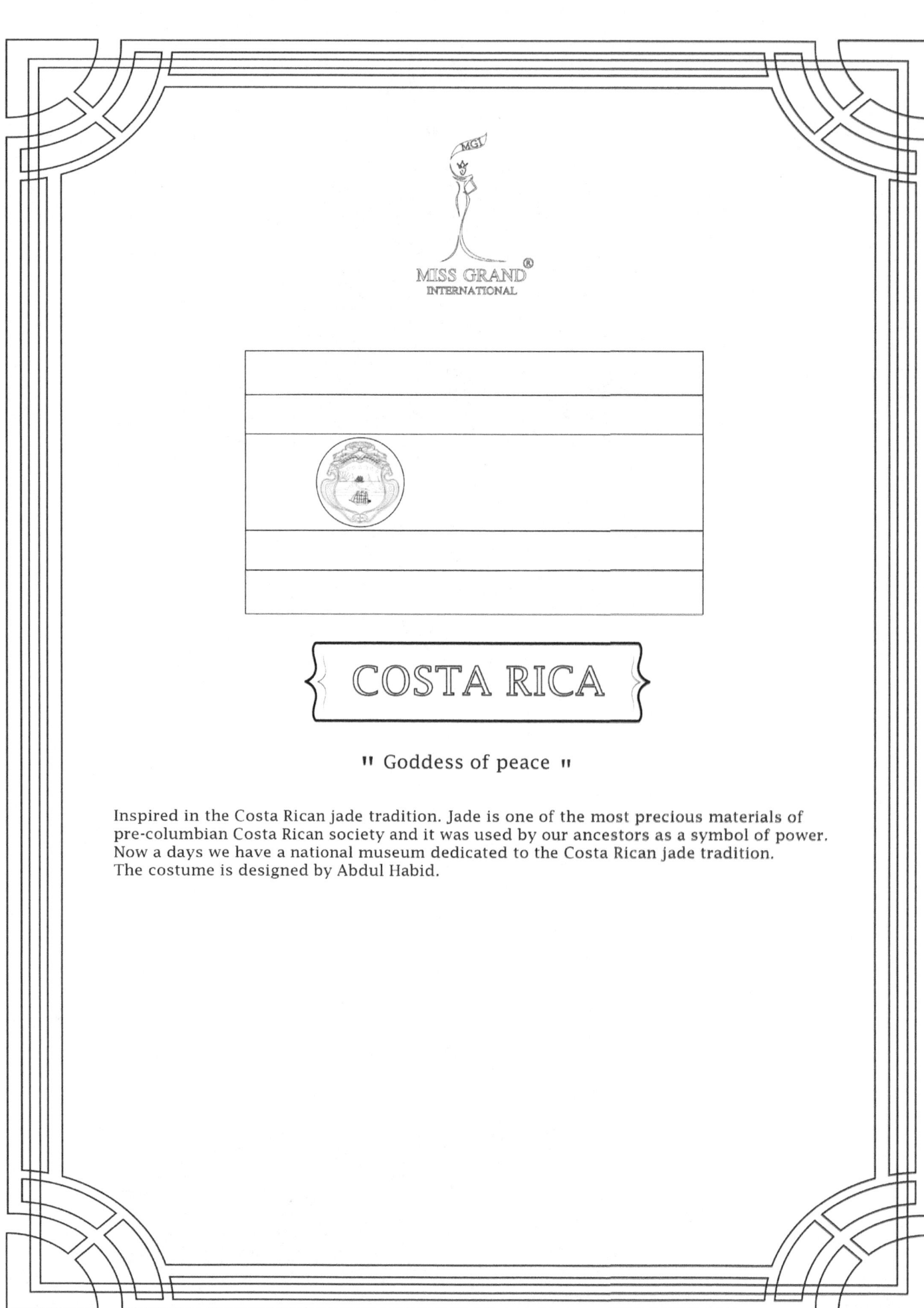

COSTA RICA

" Goddess of peace "

Inspired in the Costa Rican jade tradition. Jade is one of the most precious materials of pre-columbian Costa Rican society and it was used by our ancestors as a symbol of power. Now a days we have a national museum dedicated to the Costa Rican jade tradition.
The costume is designed by Abdul Habid.

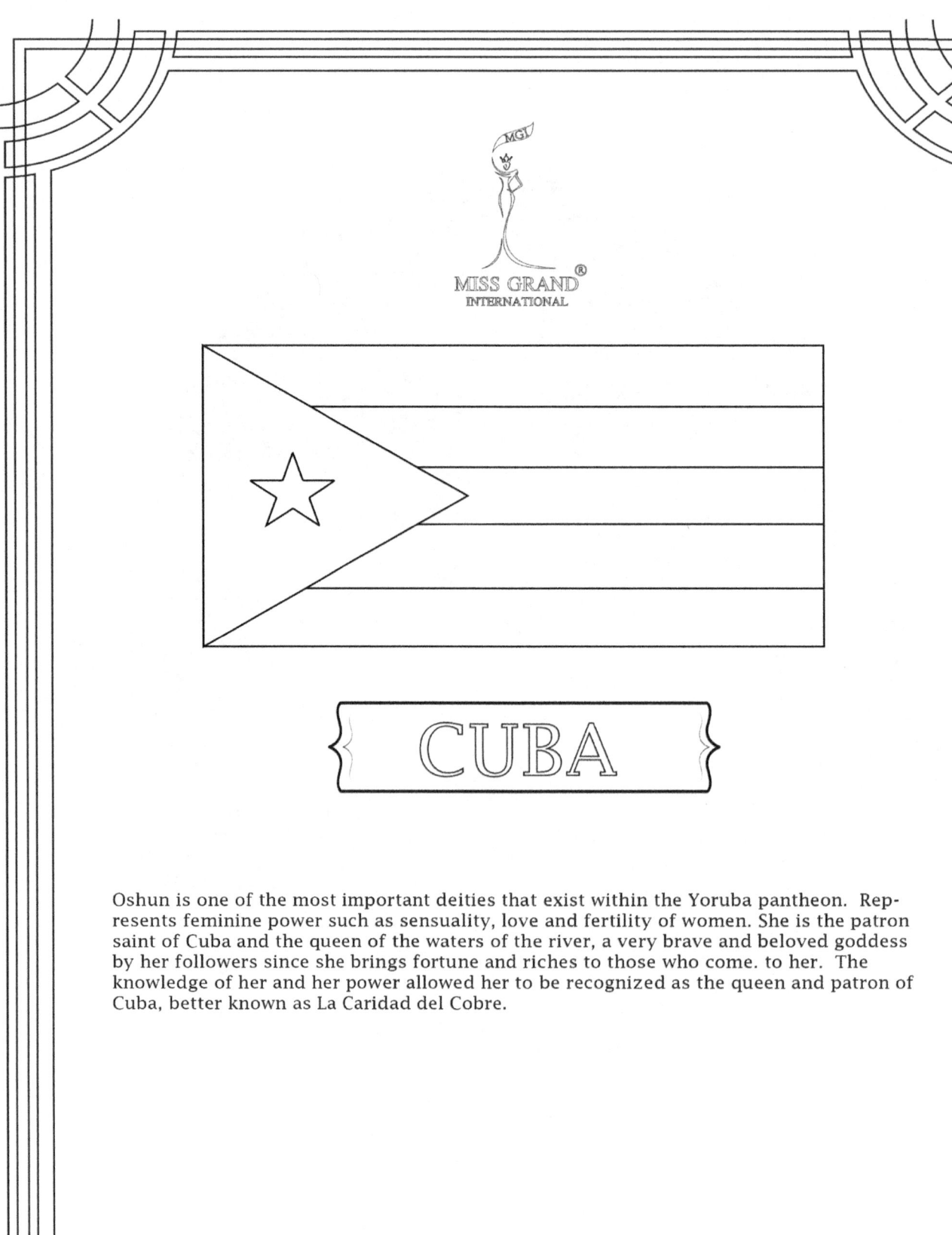

Oshun is one of the most important deities that exist within the Yoruba pantheon. Represents feminine power such as sensuality, love and fertility of women. She is the patron saint of Cuba and the queen of the waters of the river, a very brave and beloved goddess by her followers since she brings fortune and riches to those who come. to her. The knowledge of her and her power allowed her to be recognized as the queen and patron of Cuba, better known as La Caridad del Cobre.

The designer conveys our relationship to the windmills to each of our lives in order to make humankind realize that we are all equal, life flows through each and everyone of us because we all breathe the same air.

Our powerful and steady wind is the provider of the necessary spin that is needed for execution of the windmill. The wind is a symbol of our fighting spirit and it is the vital breath of our planet.

The wind is powerful, invisible, but we can all feel its effects because our windmills have become imperative for distribution of water and generation of electricity, the elements that are vital for everyone who lives on earth.

Inspiration :
The inspiration for this fantasy has been the windmills on the Island of Curaçao that have been in use for centuries to pump water on Curaçao. The windfarms on Curaçao are

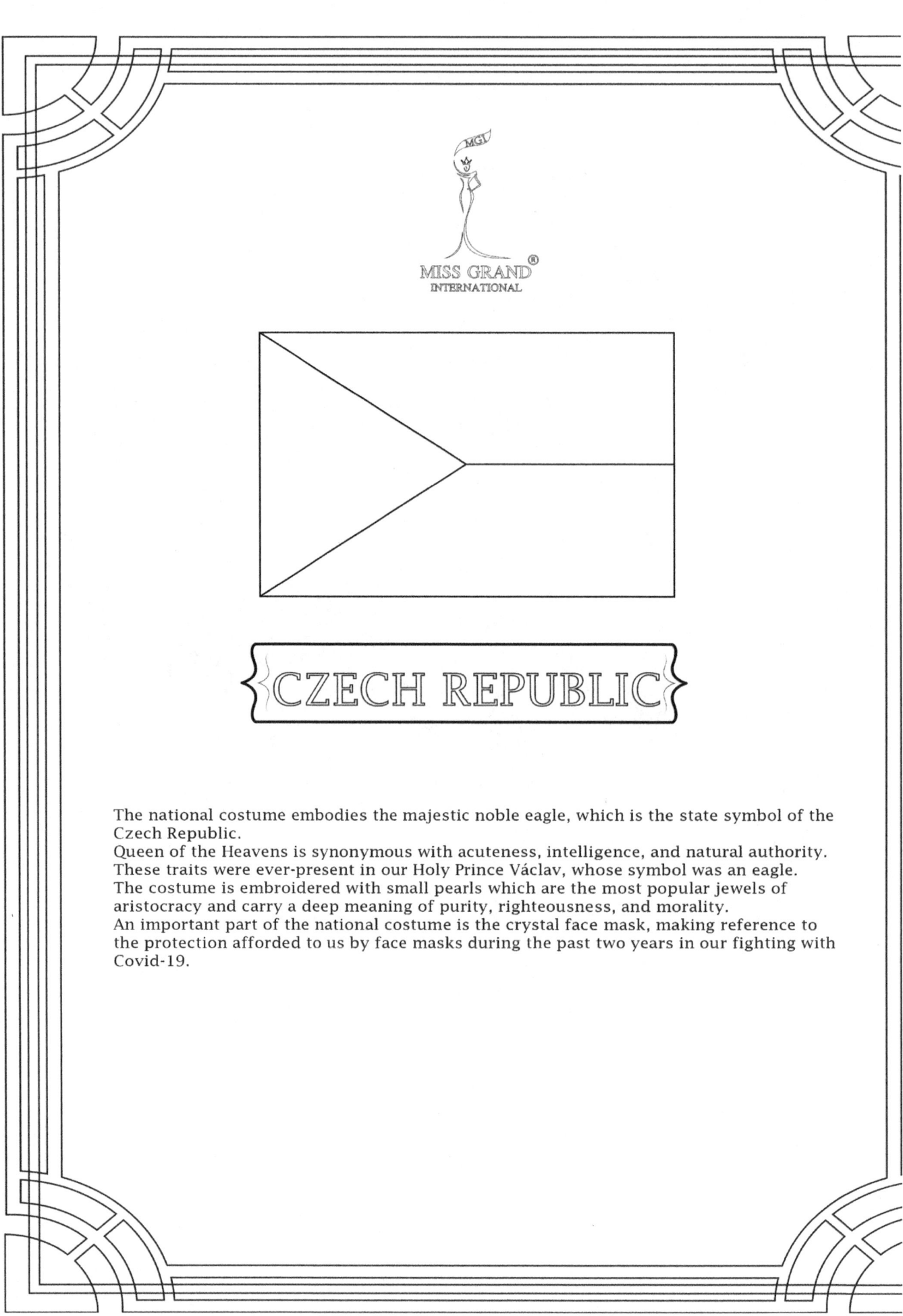

CZECH REPUBLIC

The national costume embodies the majestic noble eagle, which is the state symbol of the Czech Republic.
Queen of the Heavens is synonymous with acuteness, intelligence, and natural authority. These traits were ever-present in our Holy Prince Václav, whose symbol was an eagle.
The costume is embroidered with small pearls which are the most popular jewels of aristocracy and carry a deep meaning of purity, righteousness, and morality.
An important part of the national costume is the crystal face mask, making reference to the protection afforded to us by face masks during the past two years in our fighting with Covid-19.

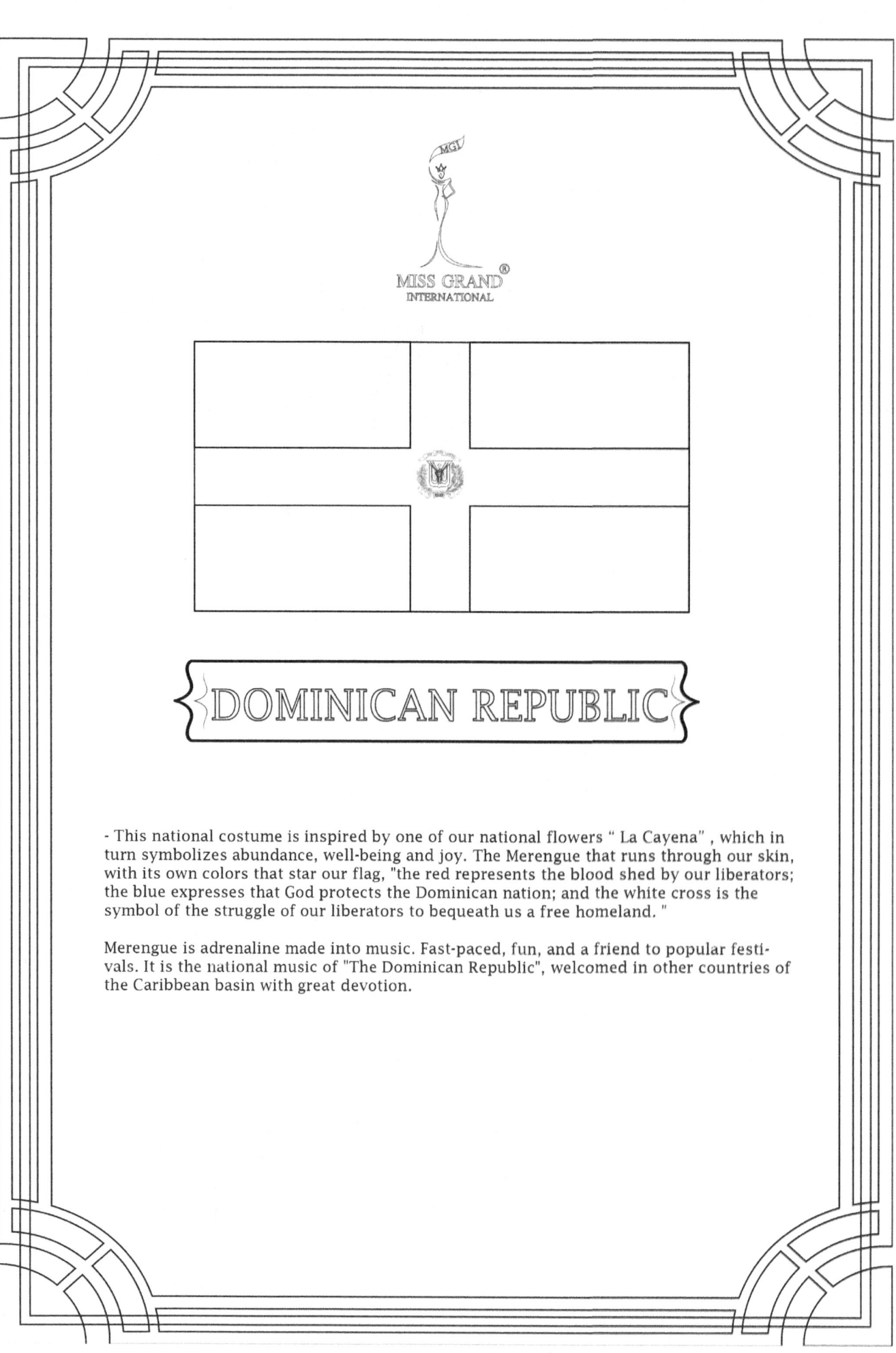

DOMINICAN REPUBLIC

- This national costume is inspired by one of our national flowers " La Cayena", which in turn symbolizes abundance, well-being and joy. The Merengue that runs through our skin, with its own colors that star our flag, "the red represents the blood shed by our liberators; the blue expresses that God protects the Dominican nation; and the white cross is the symbol of the struggle of our liberators to bequeath us a free homeland."

Merengue is adrenaline made into music. Fast-paced, fun, and a friend to popular festivals. It is the national music of "The Dominican Republic", welcomed in other countries of the Caribbean basin with great devotion.

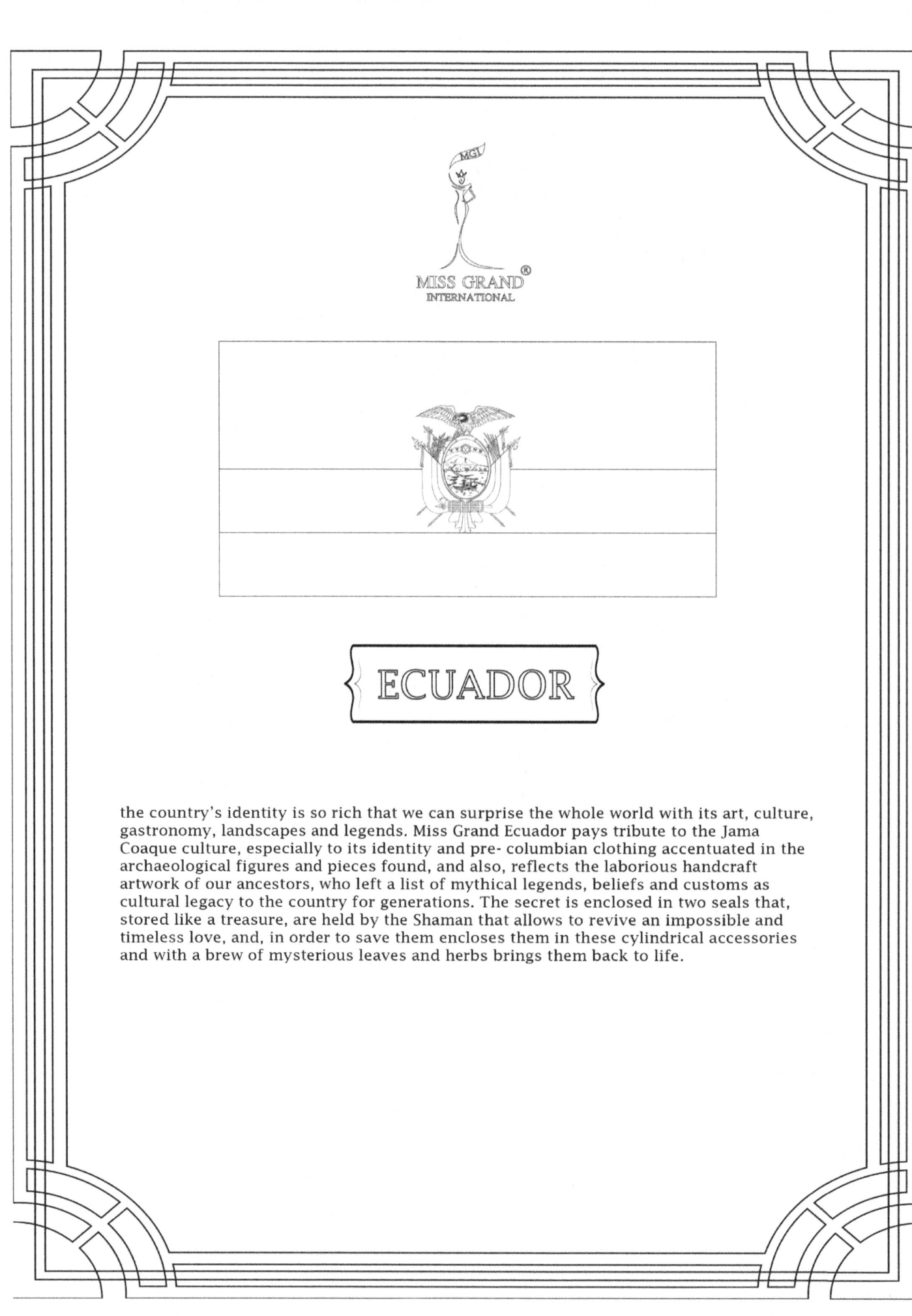

ECUADOR

the country's identity is so rich that we can surprise the whole world with its art, culture, gastronomy, landscapes and legends. Miss Grand Ecuador pays tribute to the Jama Coaque culture, especially to its identity and pre- columbian clothing accentuated in the archaeological figures and pieces found, and also, reflects the laborious handcraft artwork of our ancestors, who left a list of mythical legends, beliefs and customs as cultural legacy to the country for generations. The secret is enclosed in two seals that, stored like a treasure, are held by the Shaman that allows to revive an impossible and timeless love, and, in order to save them encloses them in these cylindrical accessories and with a brew of mysterious leaves and herbs brings them back to life.

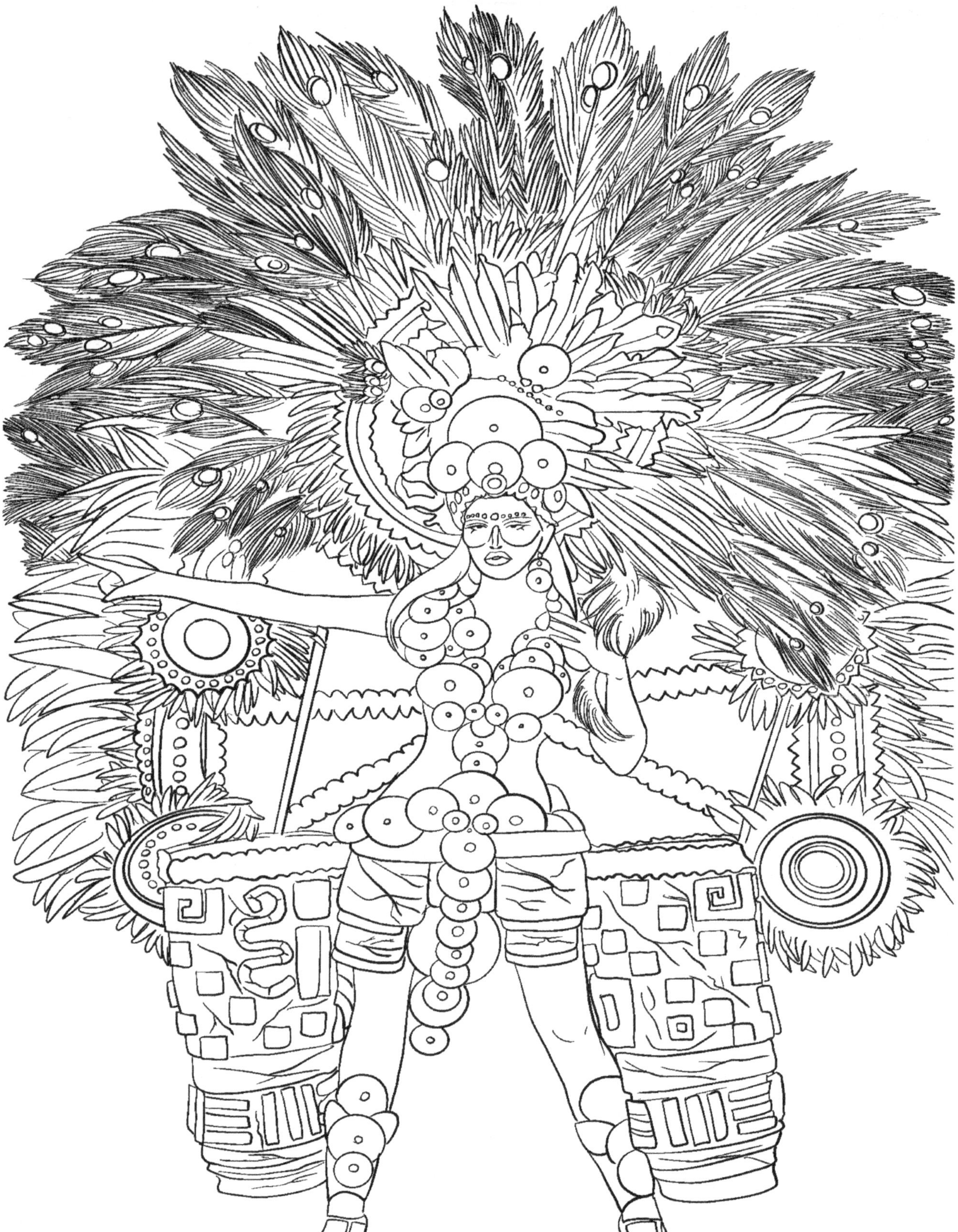

EGYPT

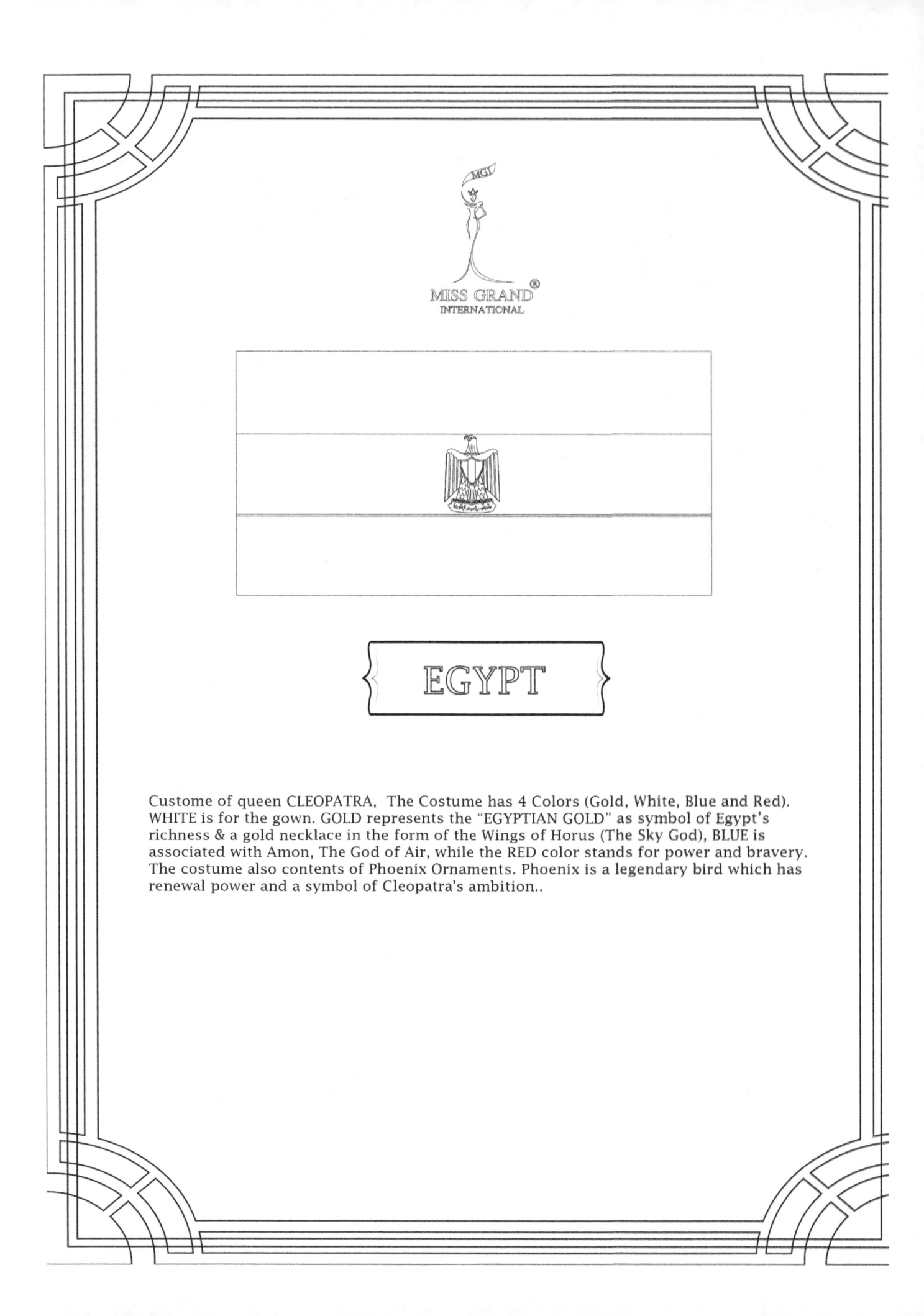

Custome of queen CLEOPATRA, The Costume has 4 Colors (Gold, White, Blue and Red). WHITE is for the gown. GOLD represents the "EGYPTIAN GOLD" as symbol of Egypt's richness & a gold necklace in the form of the Wings of Horus (The Sky God), BLUE is associated with Amon, The God of Air, while the RED color stands for power and bravery. The costume also contents of Phoenix Ornaments. Phoenix is a legendary bird which has renewal power and a symbol of Cleopatra's ambition..

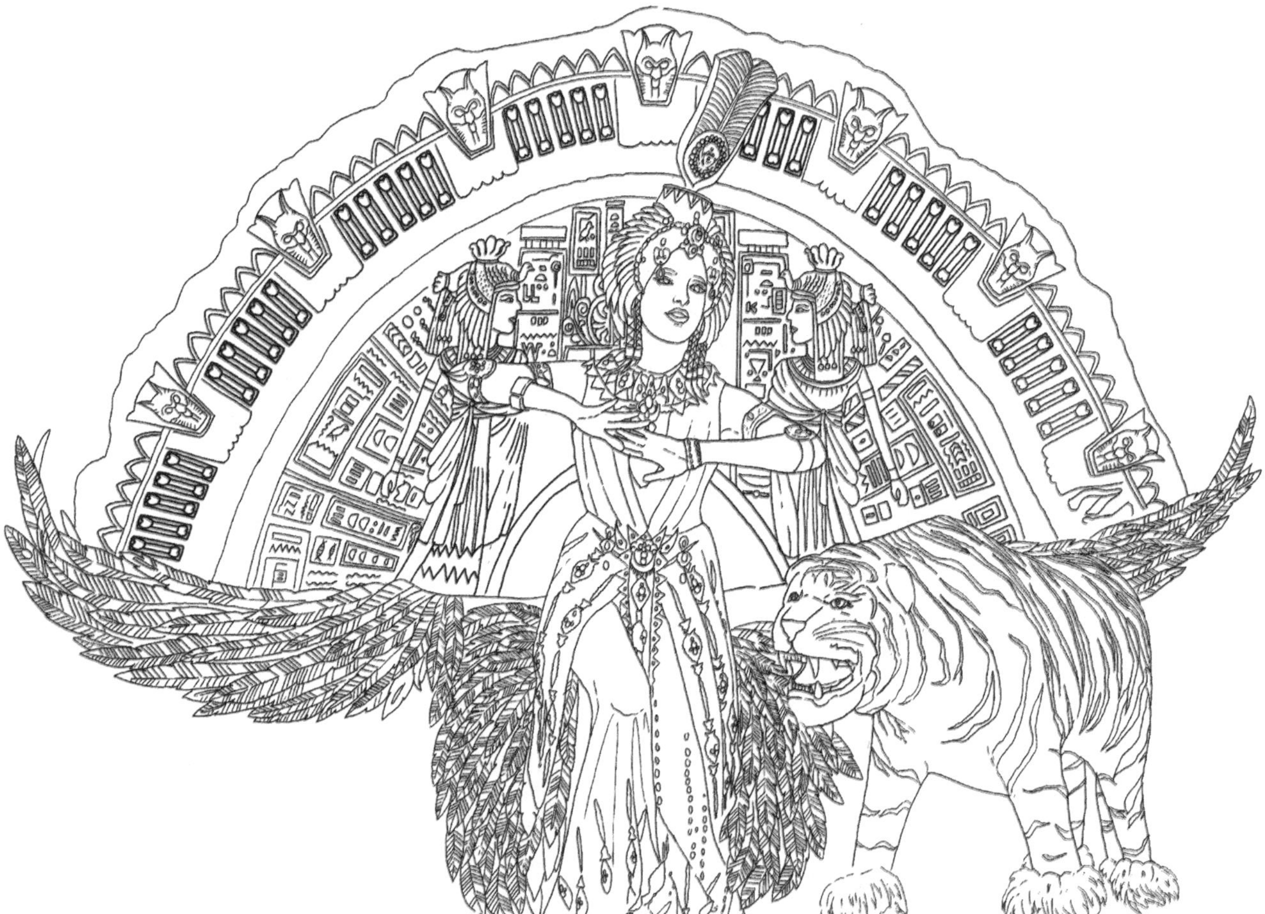

EL SALVADOR

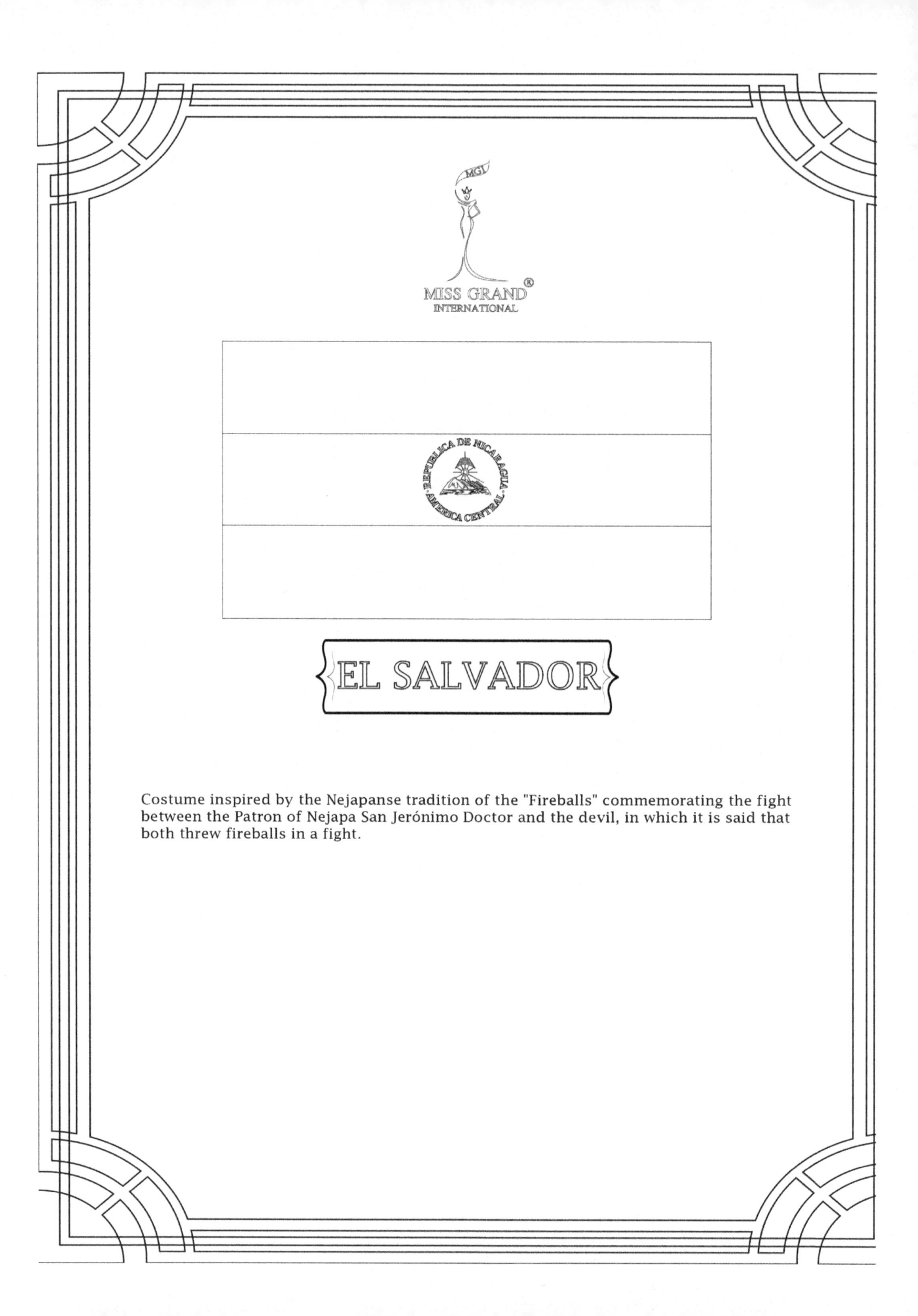

Costume inspired by the Nejapanse tradition of the "Fireballs" commemorating the fight between the Patron of Nejapa San Jerónimo Doctor and the devil, in which it is said that both threw fireballs in a fight.

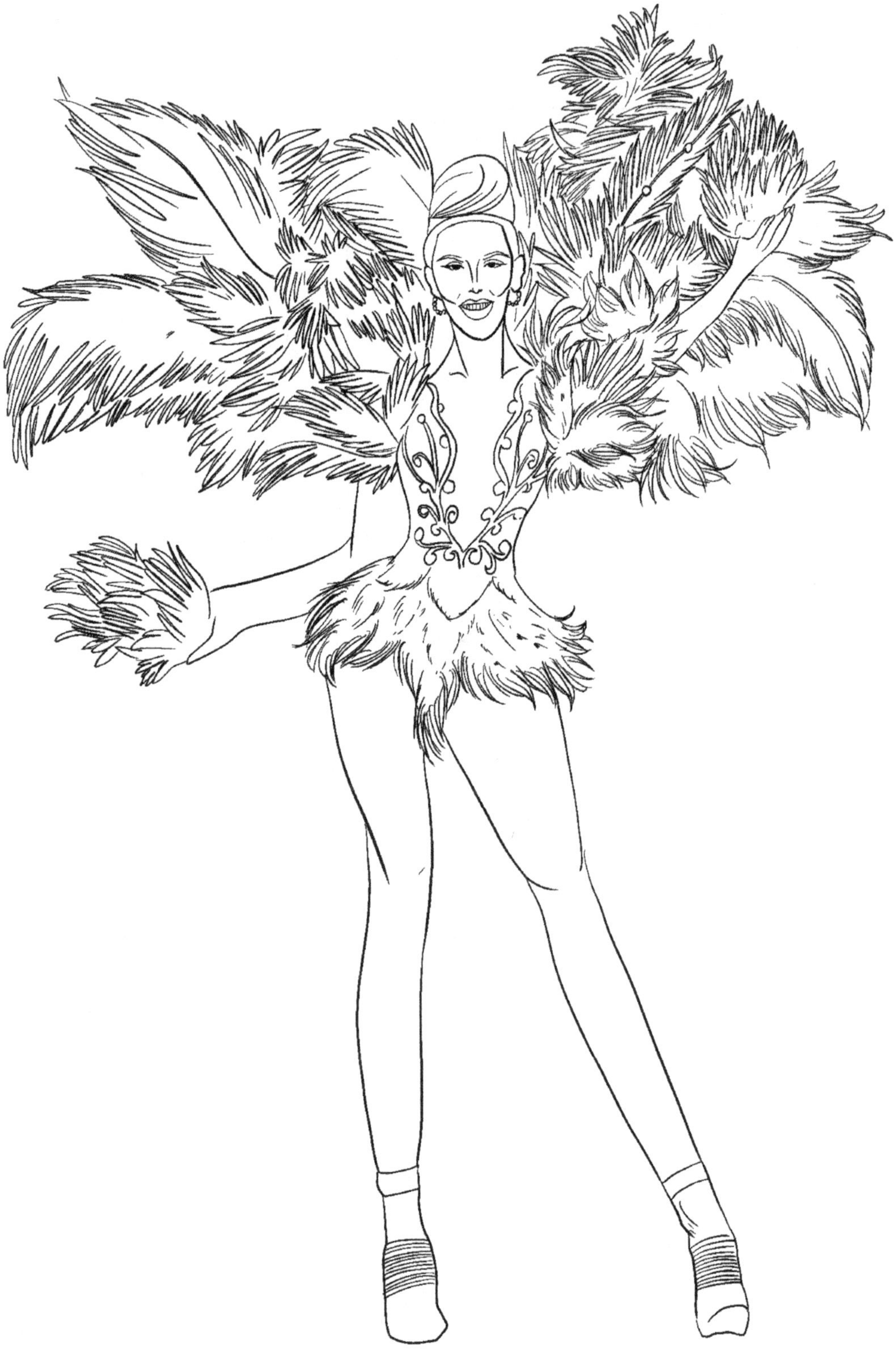

MISS GRAND
INTERNATIONAL

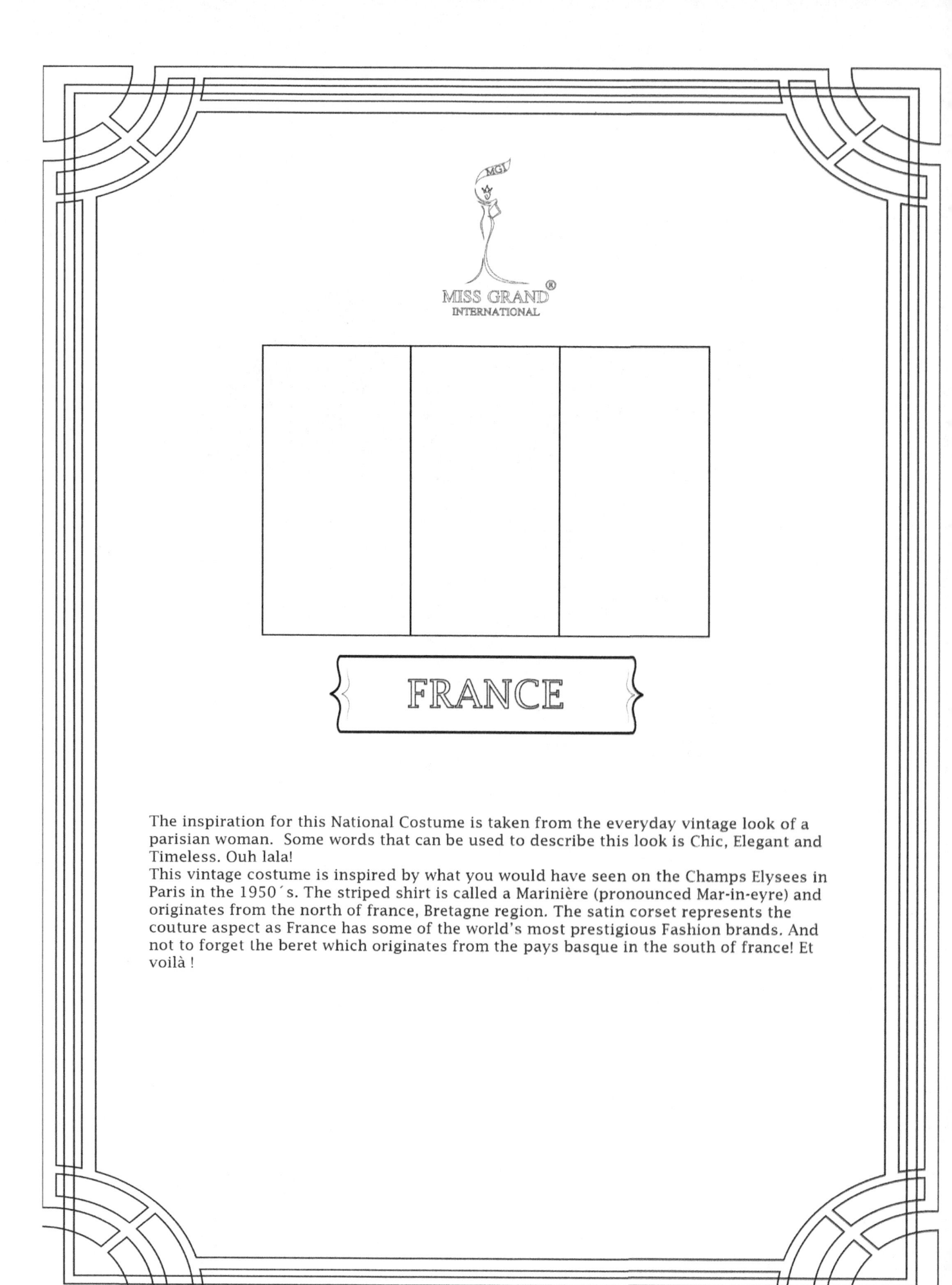

{ FRANCE }

The inspiration for this National Costume is taken from the everyday vintage look of a parisian woman. Some words that can be used to describe this look is Chic, Elegant and Timeless. Ouh lala!
This vintage costume is inspired by what you would have seen on the Champs Elysees in Paris in the 1950´s. The striped shirt is called a Marinière (pronounced Mar-in-eyre) and originates from the north of france, Bretagne region. The satin corset represents the couture aspect as France has some of the world's most prestigious Fashion brands. And not to forget the beret which originates from the pays basque in the south of france! Et voilà !

GERMANY

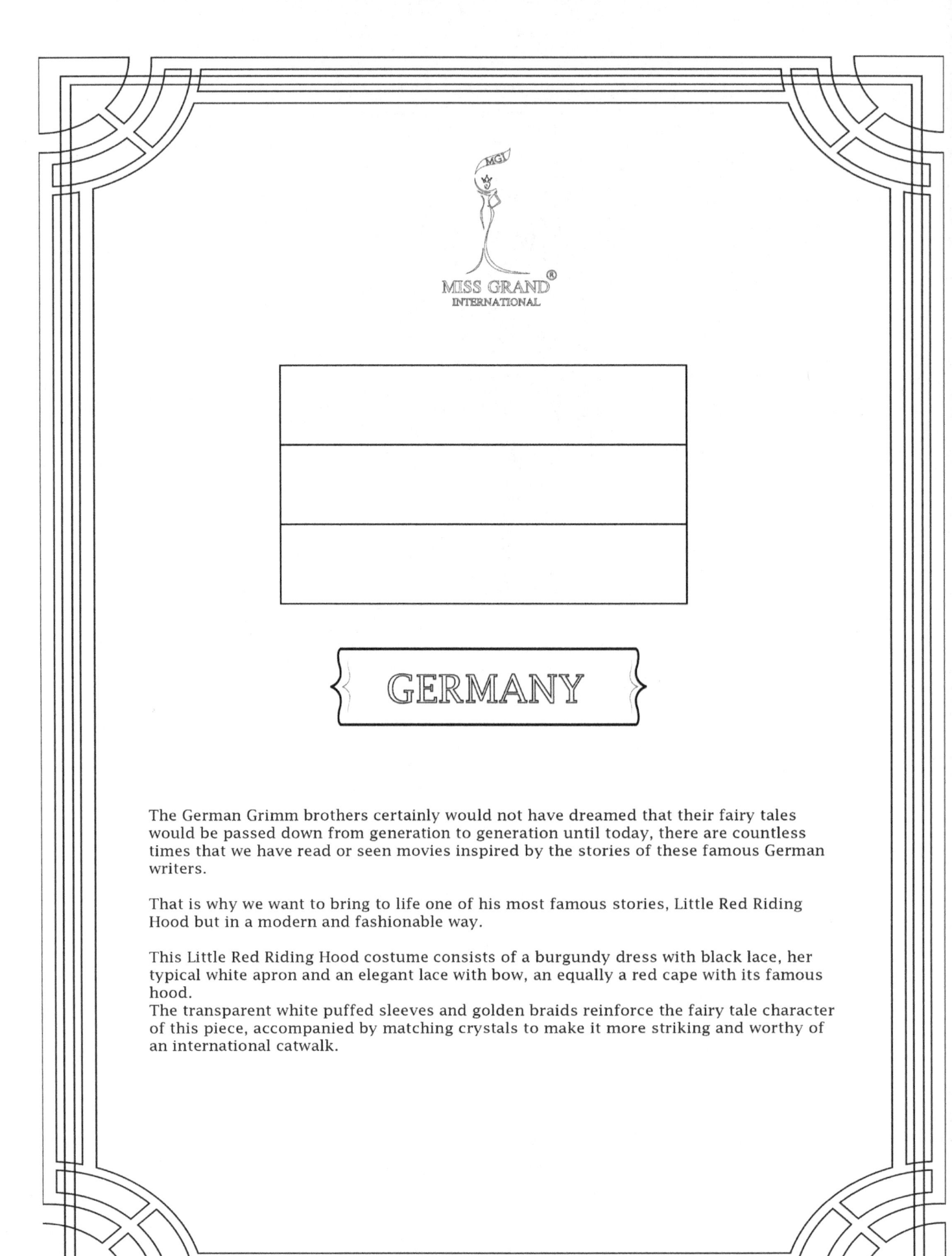

The German Grimm brothers certainly would not have dreamed that their fairy tales would be passed down from generation to generation until today, there are countless times that we have read or seen movies inspired by the stories of these famous German writers.

That is why we want to bring to life one of his most famous stories, Little Red Riding Hood but in a modern and fashionable way.

This Little Red Riding Hood costume consists of a burgundy dress with black lace, her typical white apron and an elegant lace with bow, an equally a red cape with its famous hood.
The transparent white puffed sleeves and golden braids reinforce the fairy tale character of this piece, accompanied by matching crystals to make it more striking and worthy of an international catwalk.

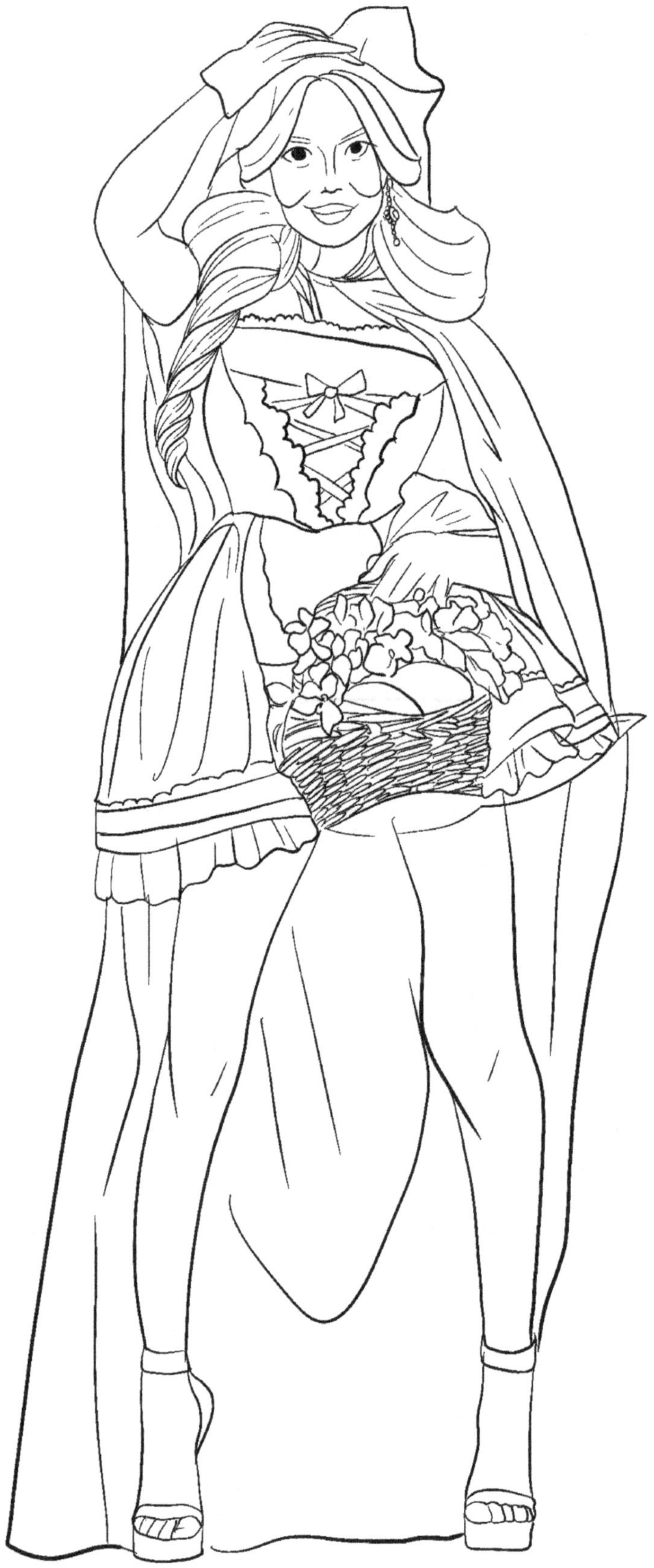

GUATEMALA

GODDESS IXCHEL

The suit features a handmade textile made by artists from the Guatemalan highlands. Embroidered with bohemian glass and wood beads, it imitates details of ancient Mayan costumes. The headdress shows Q'uq'umatz, a feathered serpent, described in the Popol Vuh as the creative entity, according to the Quiché tradition, with Ixchel being its muse. Adorned with reliefs of Mayan iconography, the back simulates a cascade of quetzal feathers, the symbolic bird of Guatemala.GODDESS IXCHEL

The suit features a handmade textile made by artists from the Guatemalan highlands. Embroidered with bohemian glass and wood beads, it imitates details of ancient Mayan costumes. The headdress shows Q'uq'umatz, a feathered serpent, described in the Popol Vuh as the creative entity, according to the Quiché tradition, with Ixchel being its muse. Adorned with reliefs of Mayan iconography, the back simulates a cascade of quetzal feathers, the symbolic bird of Guatemala.

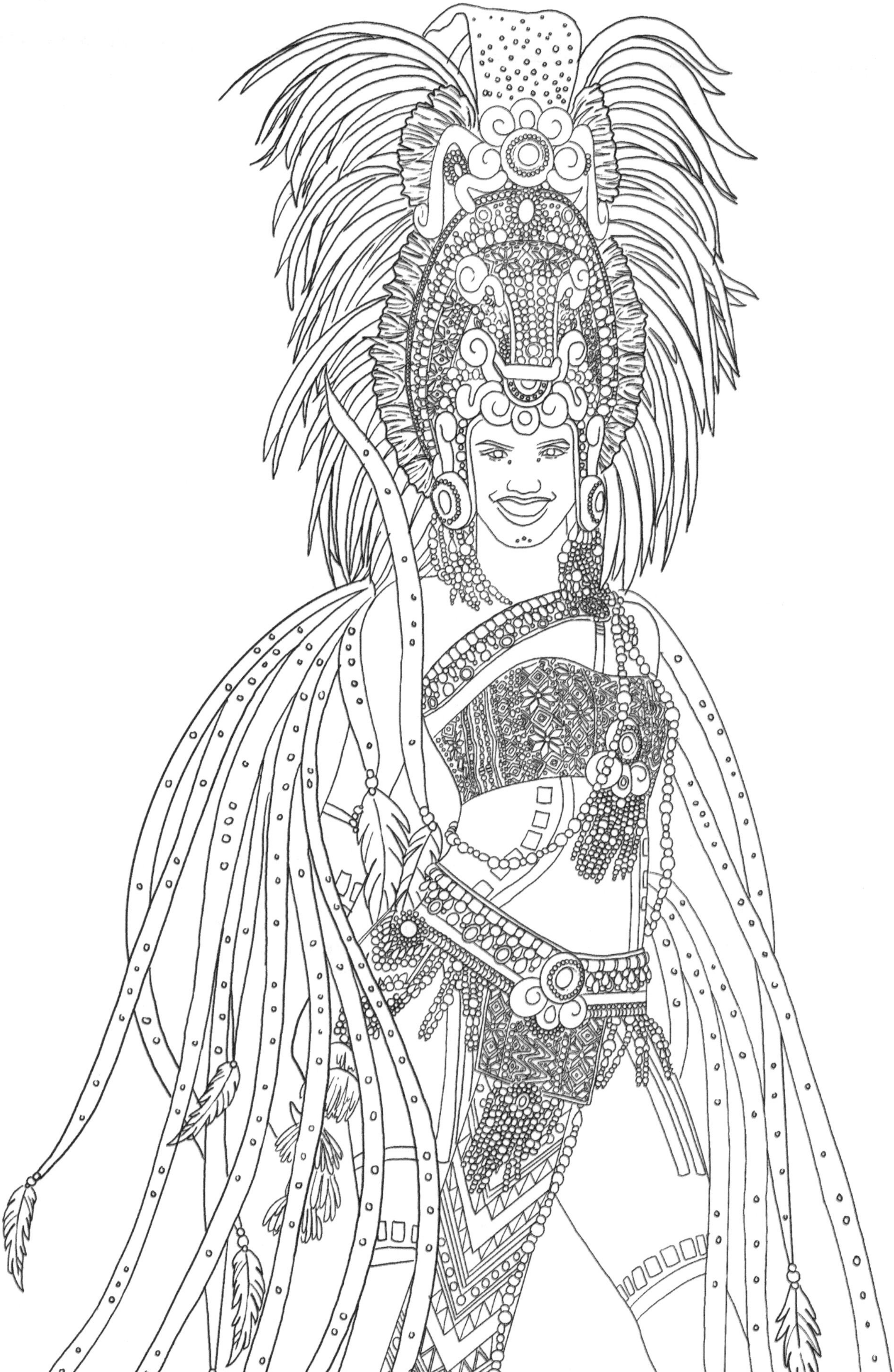

{ HAITI }

This costume portrays " Madan Sara" . " Madan Sara" is profiled as a specific type of Women in Haiti whose work is at the heart of Haiti's informal economy. Women in Haiti are deemed the pillars of their communities. They work tirelessly to buy,sell and distribute goods at their markets. Despite facing intense hardship and social stigma ,the hardwork of Madan Sara ensures a better life for generations to come .Madan Sara contributes directly to society to share their dreams for a more just Haiti.This costume also has components national symbols of Haiti , like Mango Francique, Royal Palm,Hibiscus and Karabela dress.

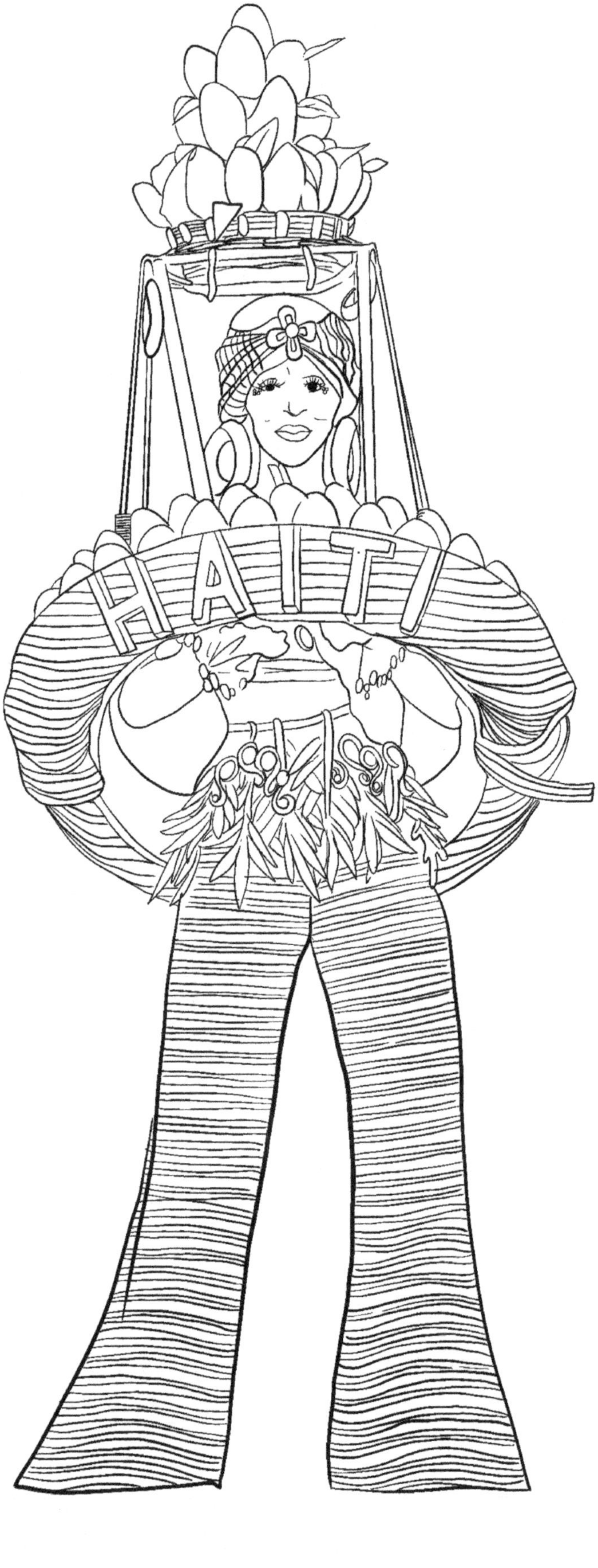
HAITI

HONDURAS

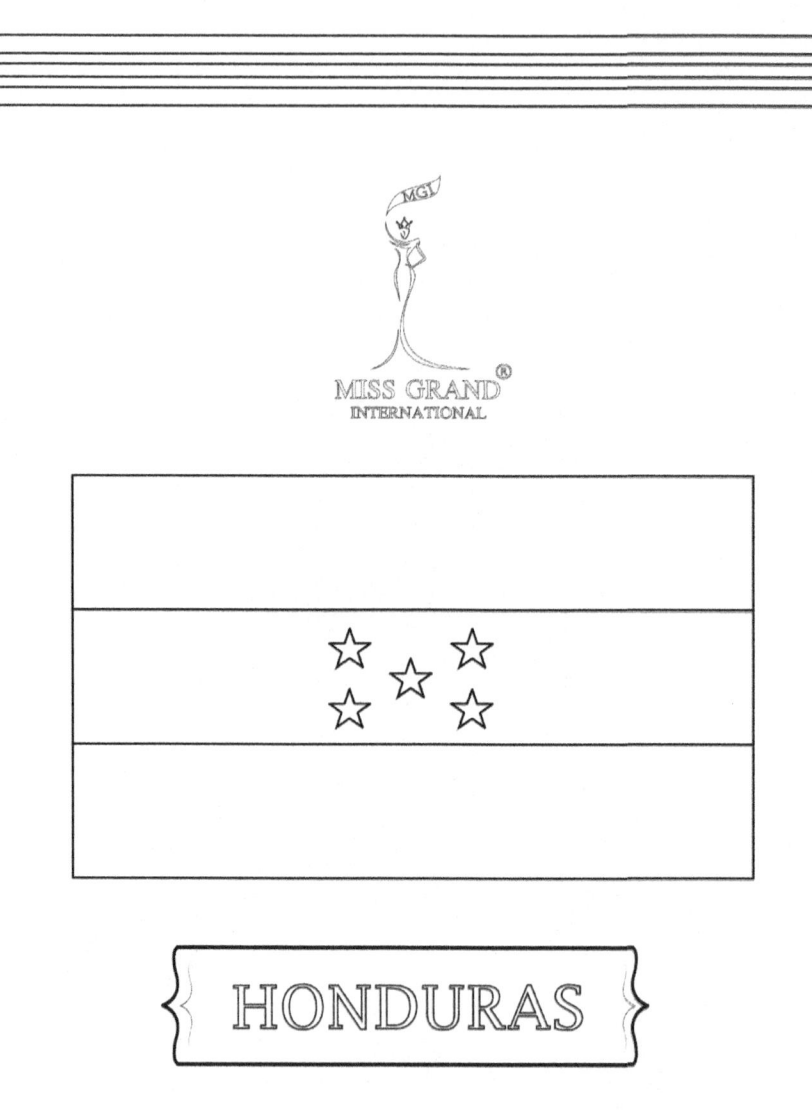

Inspired by the origin of the world, including the most influential beings of Mayan mythology, we have the jaguar God representing the power and cunning apart from being as a one of the most dangerous, it is embodied in a mesh in skin color, the eagle considered one of the most lethal and powerful warriors of the world, in the headdress we capture a triple mask where the birth of man is represented from which it arises from a corn seed, behind him the sun god, who gave energy for all living beings in the universe to grow, on the back one of the most beautiful birds of the empire, the holly Quetzal , with bing tail and beautiful feathers who highlights the beauty when its passing believed that it spread fertilizer and made the abundant harvests and that the corn fields bloomed.

it is Made with leather mesh, hand made painted , acetates, laces, metal braids, acrylic

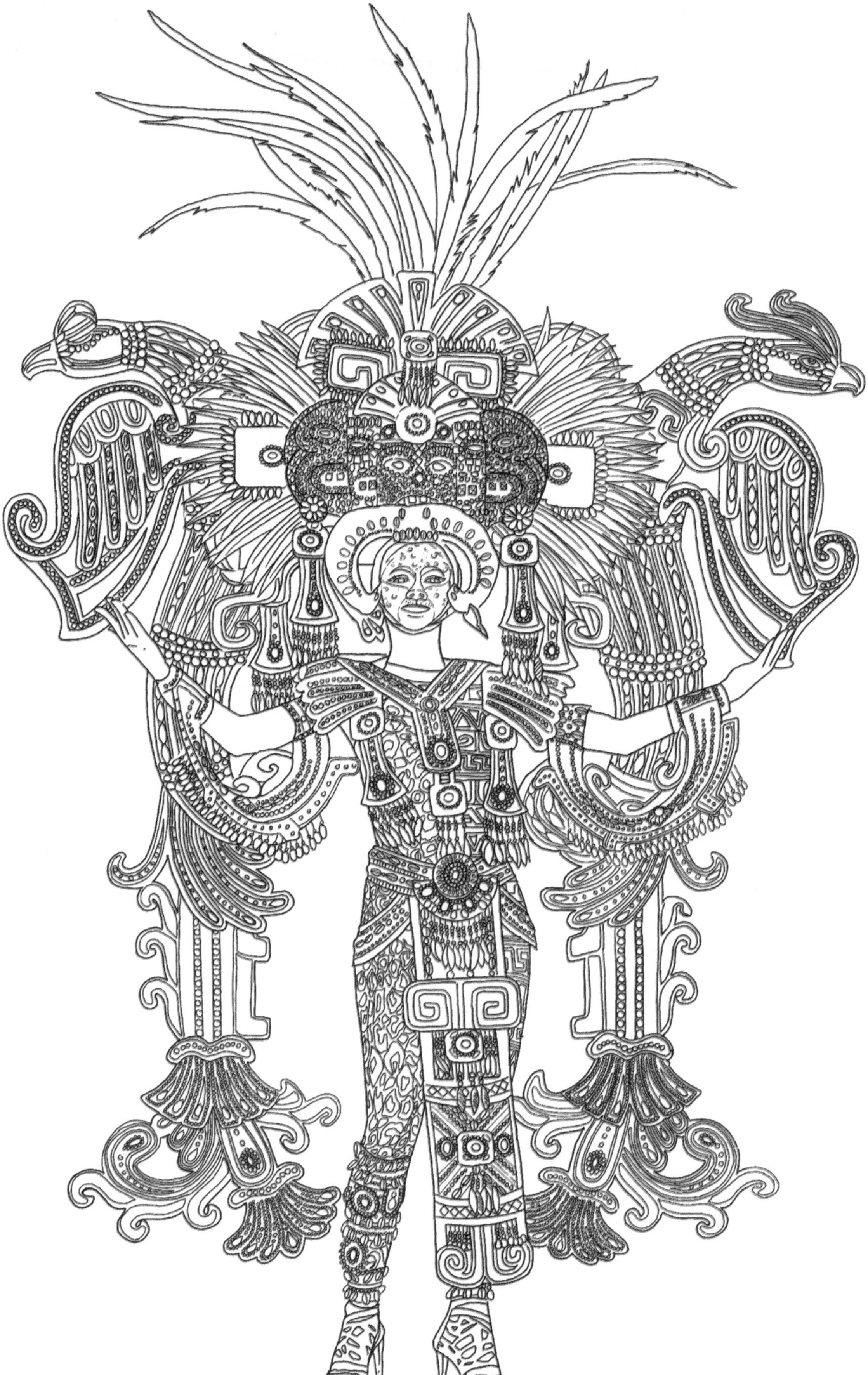

HONG KONG

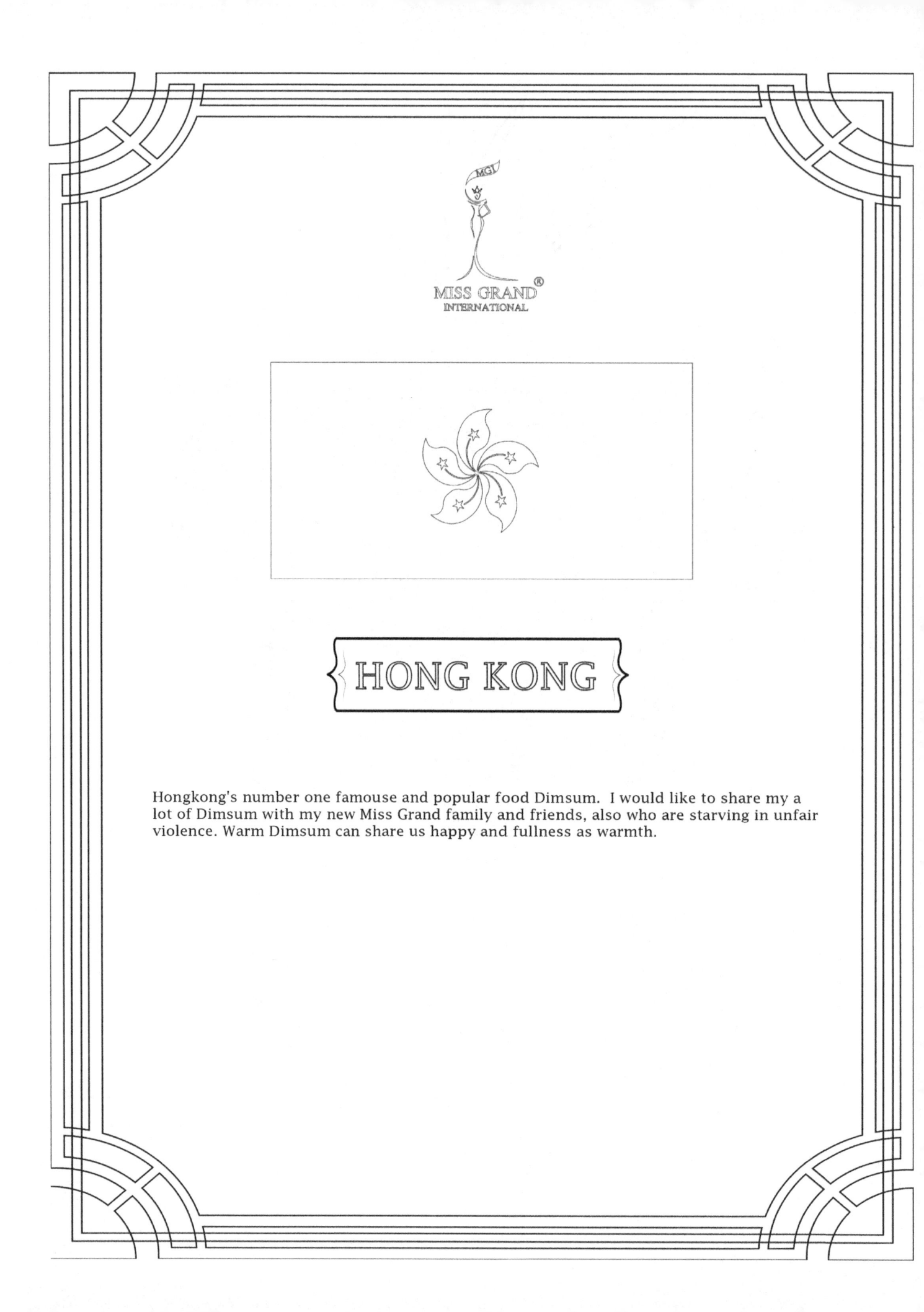

Hongkong's number one famouse and popular food Dimsum. I would like to share my a lot of Dimsum with my new Miss Grand family and friends, also who are starving in unfair violence. Warm Dimsum can share us happy and fullness as warmth.

INDIA

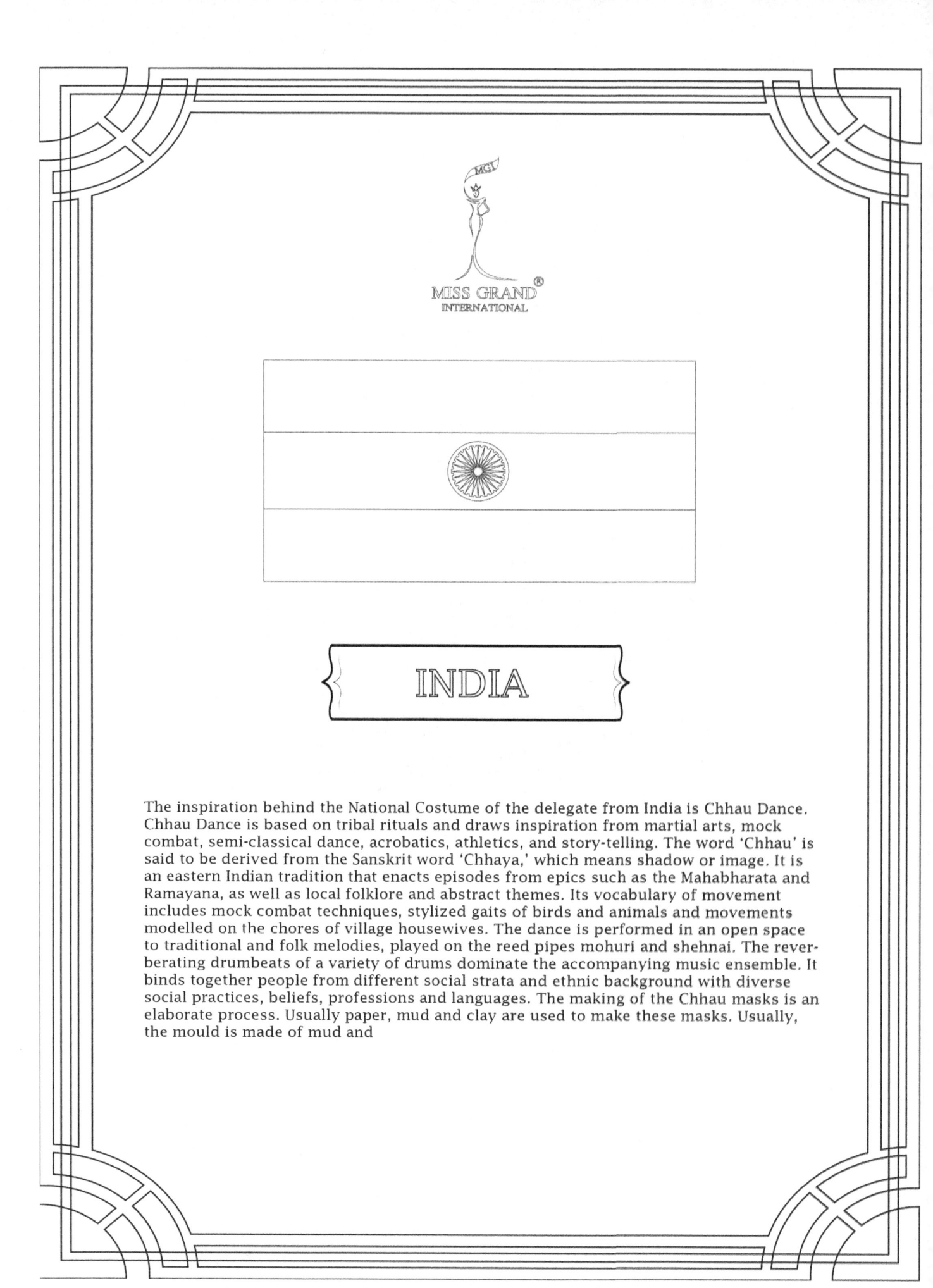

The inspiration behind the National Costume of the delegate from India is Chhau Dance. Chhau Dance is based on tribal rituals and draws inspiration from martial arts, mock combat, semi-classical dance, acrobatics, athletics, and story-telling. The word 'Chhau' is said to be derived from the Sanskrit word 'Chhaya,' which means shadow or image. It is an eastern Indian tradition that enacts episodes from epics such as the Mahabharata and Ramayana, as well as local folklore and abstract themes. Its vocabulary of movement includes mock combat techniques, stylized gaits of birds and animals and movements modelled on the chores of village housewives. The dance is performed in an open space to traditional and folk melodies, played on the reed pipes mohuri and shehnai. The reverberating drumbeats of a variety of drums dominate the accompanying music ensemble. It binds together people from different social strata and ethnic background with diverse social practices, beliefs, professions and languages. The making of the Chhau masks is an elaborate process. Usually paper, mud and clay are used to make these masks. Usually, the mould is made of mud and

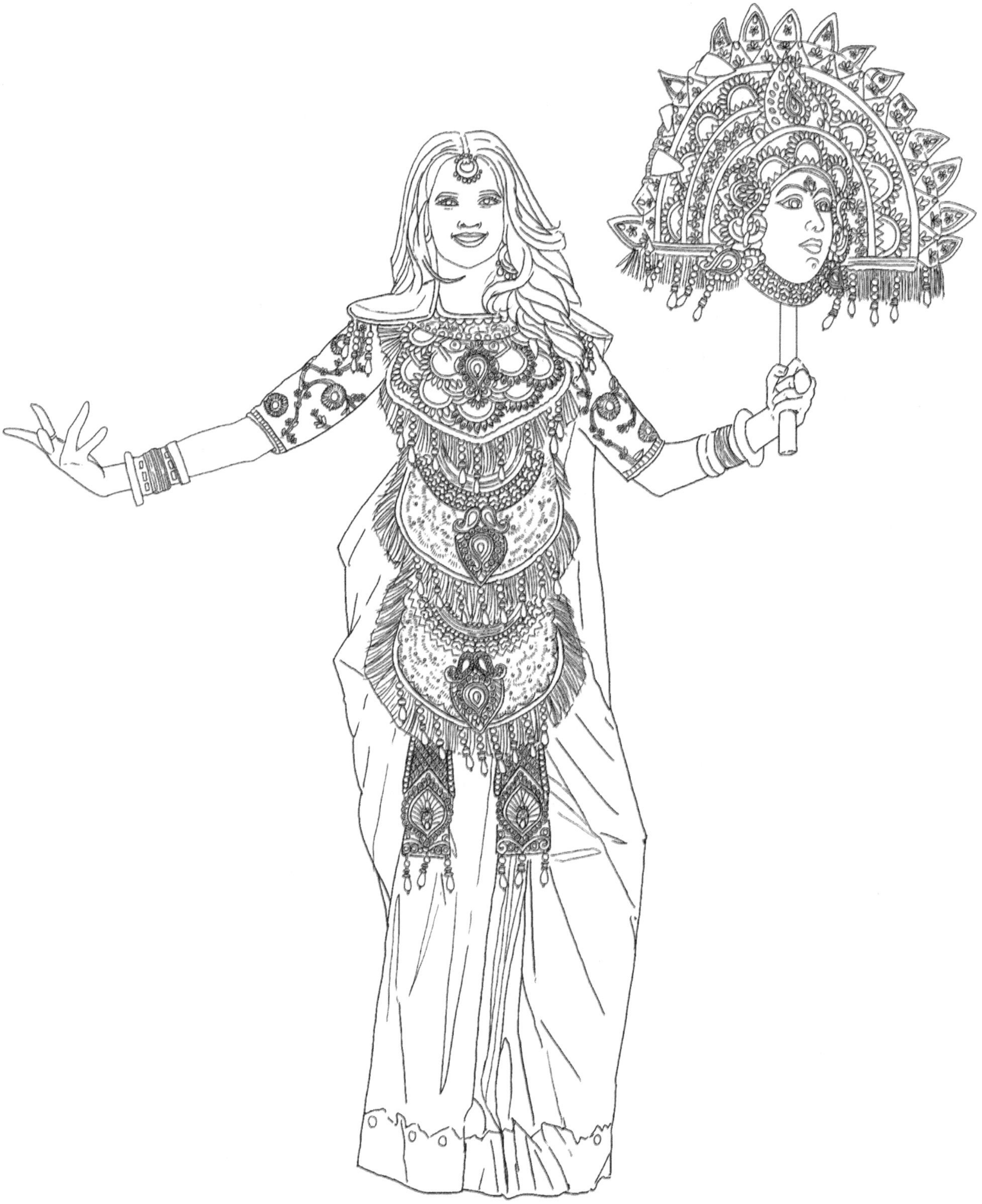

MISS GRAND INTERNATIONAL

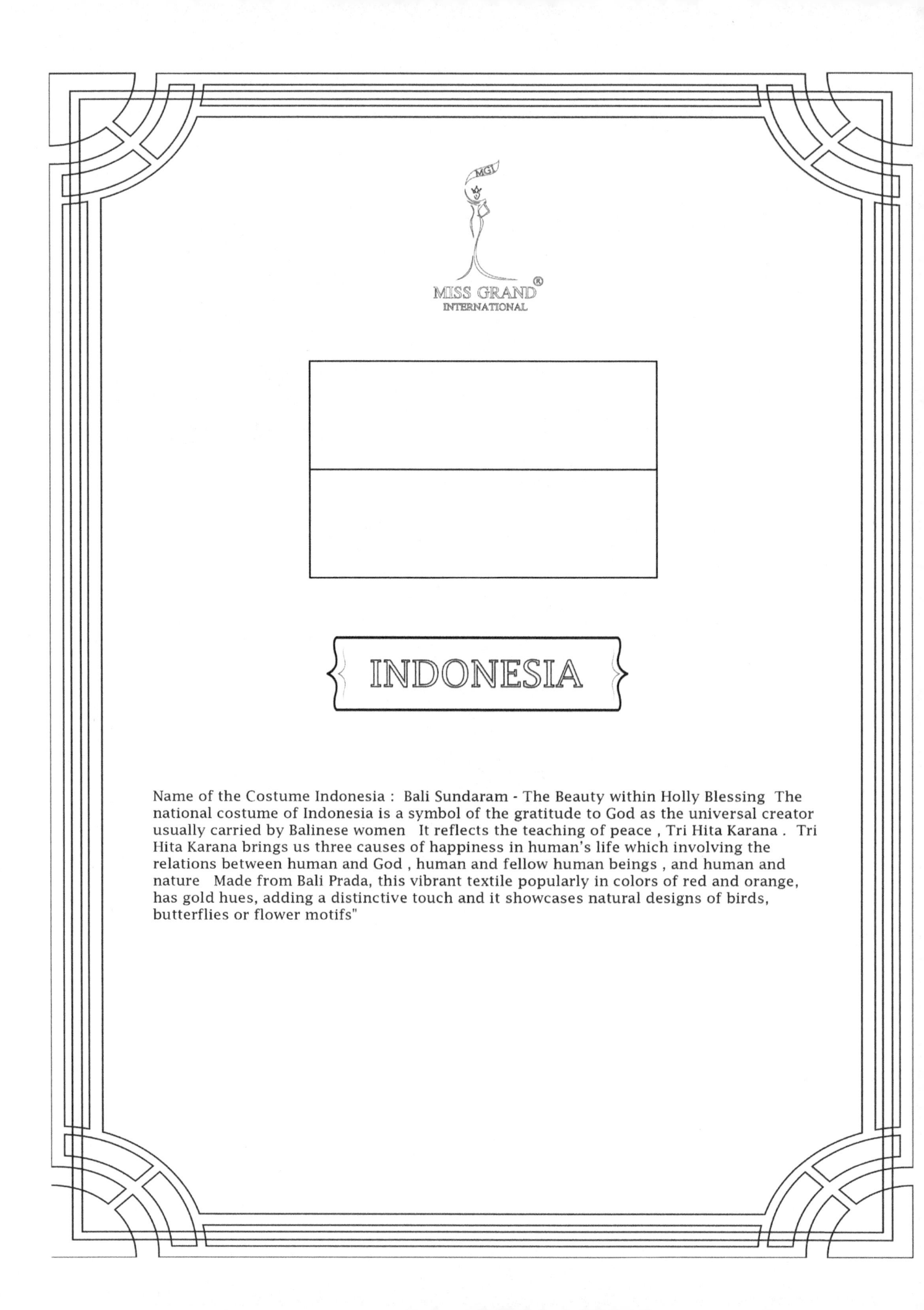

{ INDONESIA }

Name of the Costume Indonesia : Bali Sundaram - The Beauty within Holly Blessing The national costume of Indonesia is a symbol of the gratitude to God as the universal creator usually carried by Balinese women   It reflects the teaching of peace , Tri Hita Karana . Tri Hita Karana brings us three causes of happiness in human's life which involving the relations between human and God , human and fellow human beings , and human and nature   Made from Bali Prada, this vibrant textile popularly in colors of red and orange, has gold hues, adding a distinctive touch and it showcases natural designs of birds, butterflies or flower motifs"

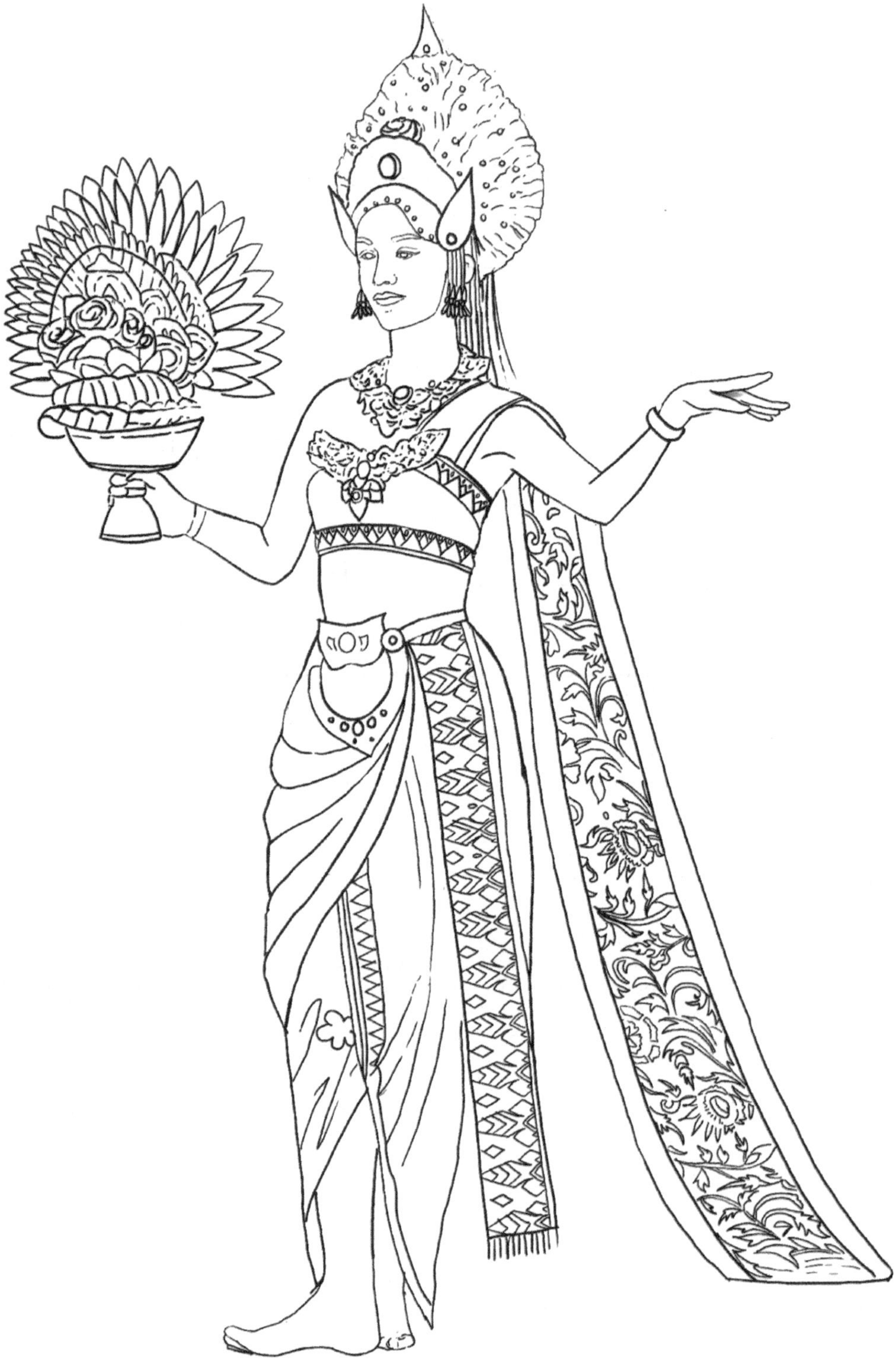

ITALY

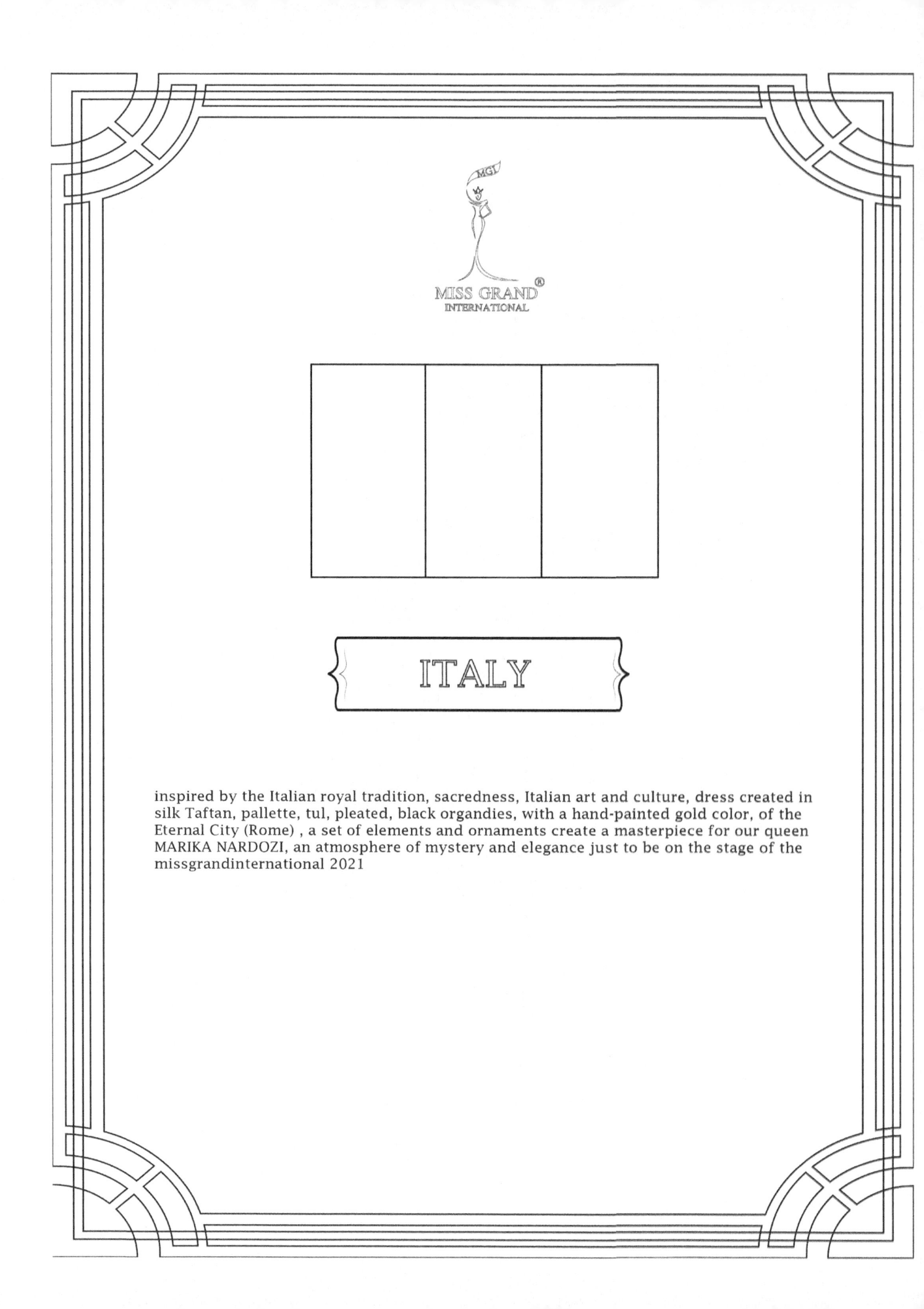

inspired by the Italian royal tradition, sacredness, Italian art and culture, dress created in silk Taftan, pallette, tul, pleated, black organdies, with a hand-painted gold color, of the Eternal City (Rome) , a set of elements and ornaments create a masterpiece for our queen MARIKA NARDOZI, an atmosphere of mystery and elegance just to be on the stage of the missgrandinternational 2021

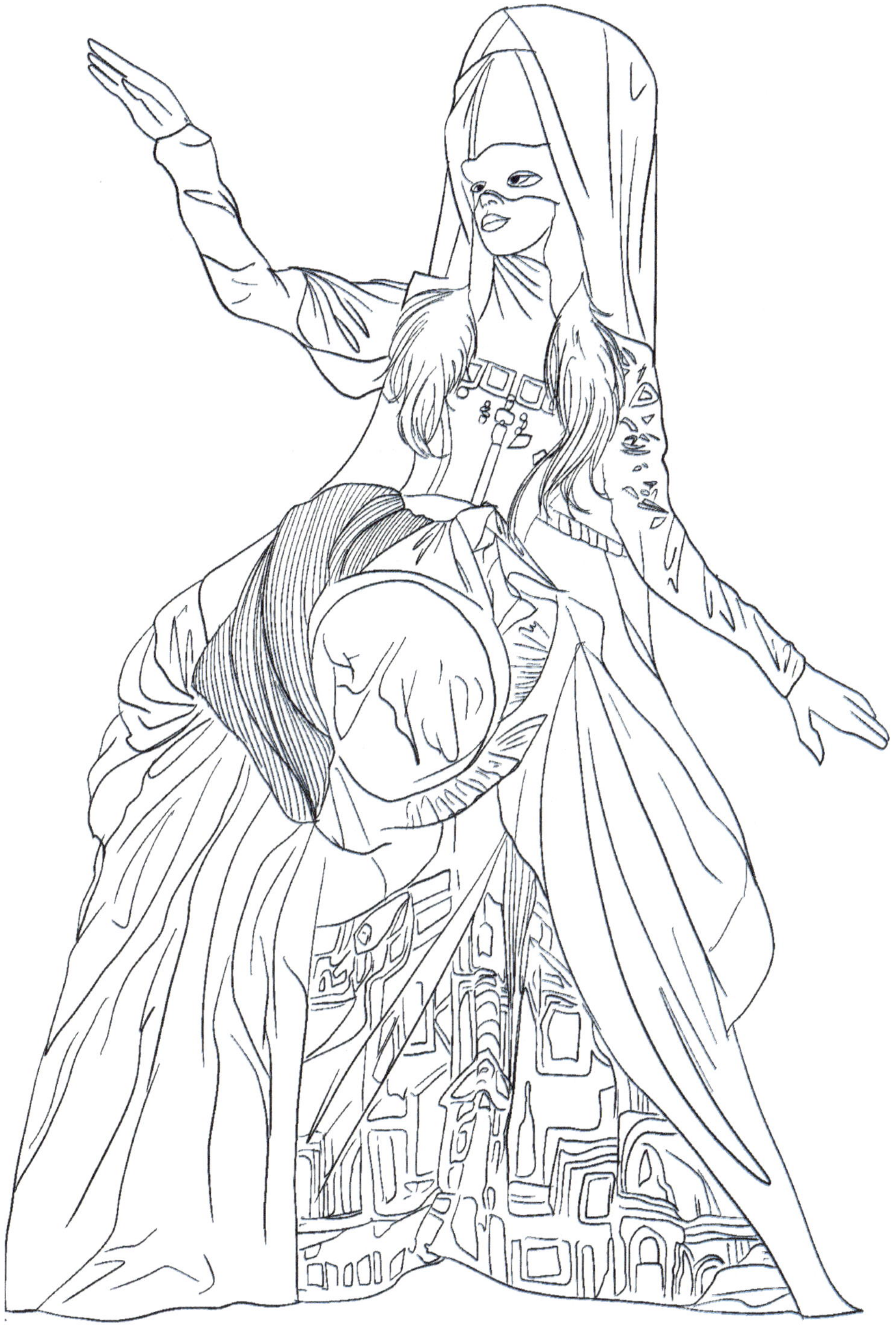

JAPAN

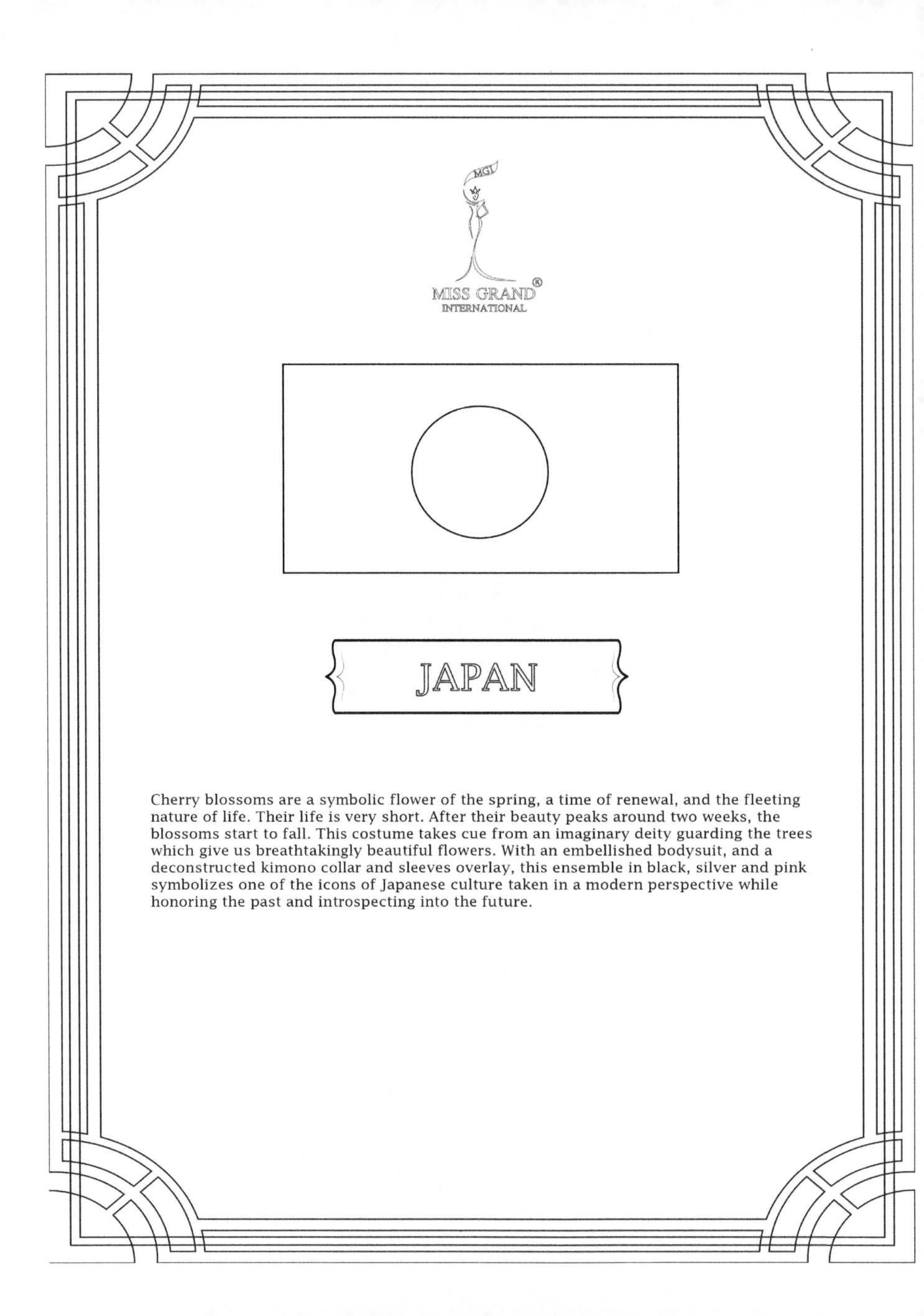

Cherry blossoms are a symbolic flower of the spring, a time of renewal, and the fleeting nature of life. Their life is very short. After their beauty peaks around two weeks, the blossoms start to fall. This costume takes cue from an imaginary deity guarding the trees which give us breathtakingly beautiful flowers. With an embellished bodysuit, and a deconstructed kimono collar and sleeves overlay, this ensemble in black, silver and pink symbolizes one of the icons of Japanese culture taken in a modern perspective while honoring the past and introspecting into the future.

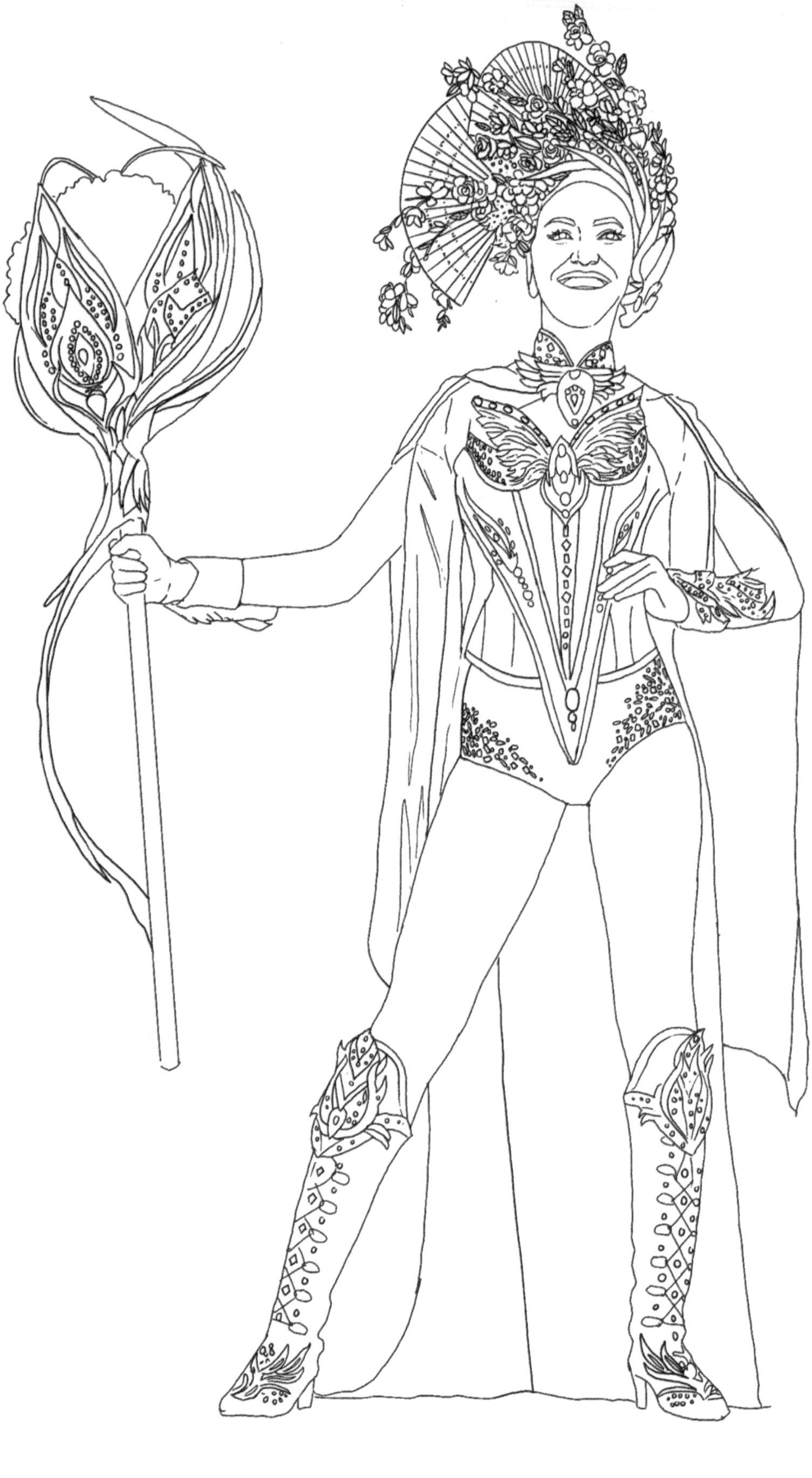

KOREA

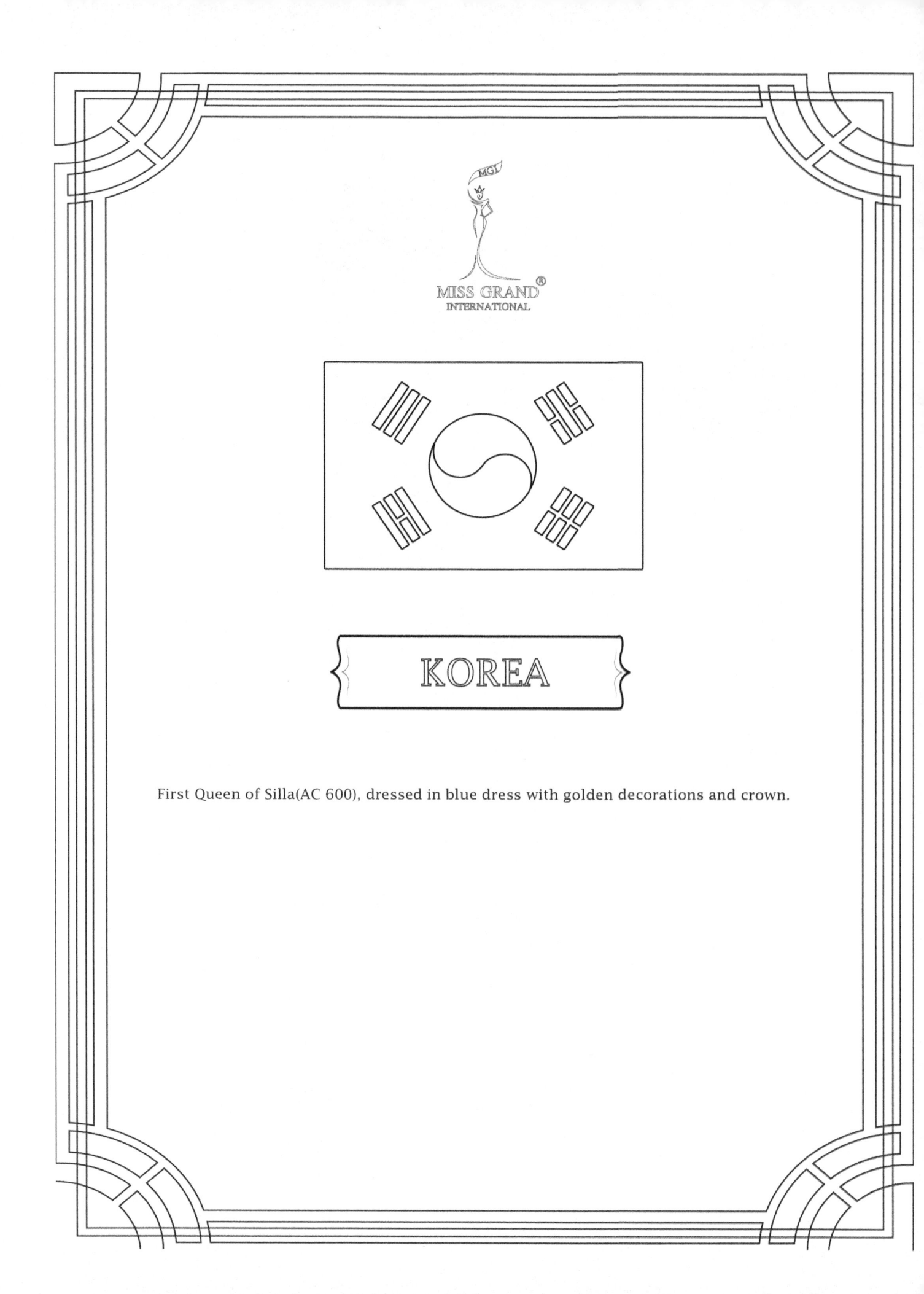

First Queen of Silla(AC 600), dressed in blue dress with golden decorations and crown.

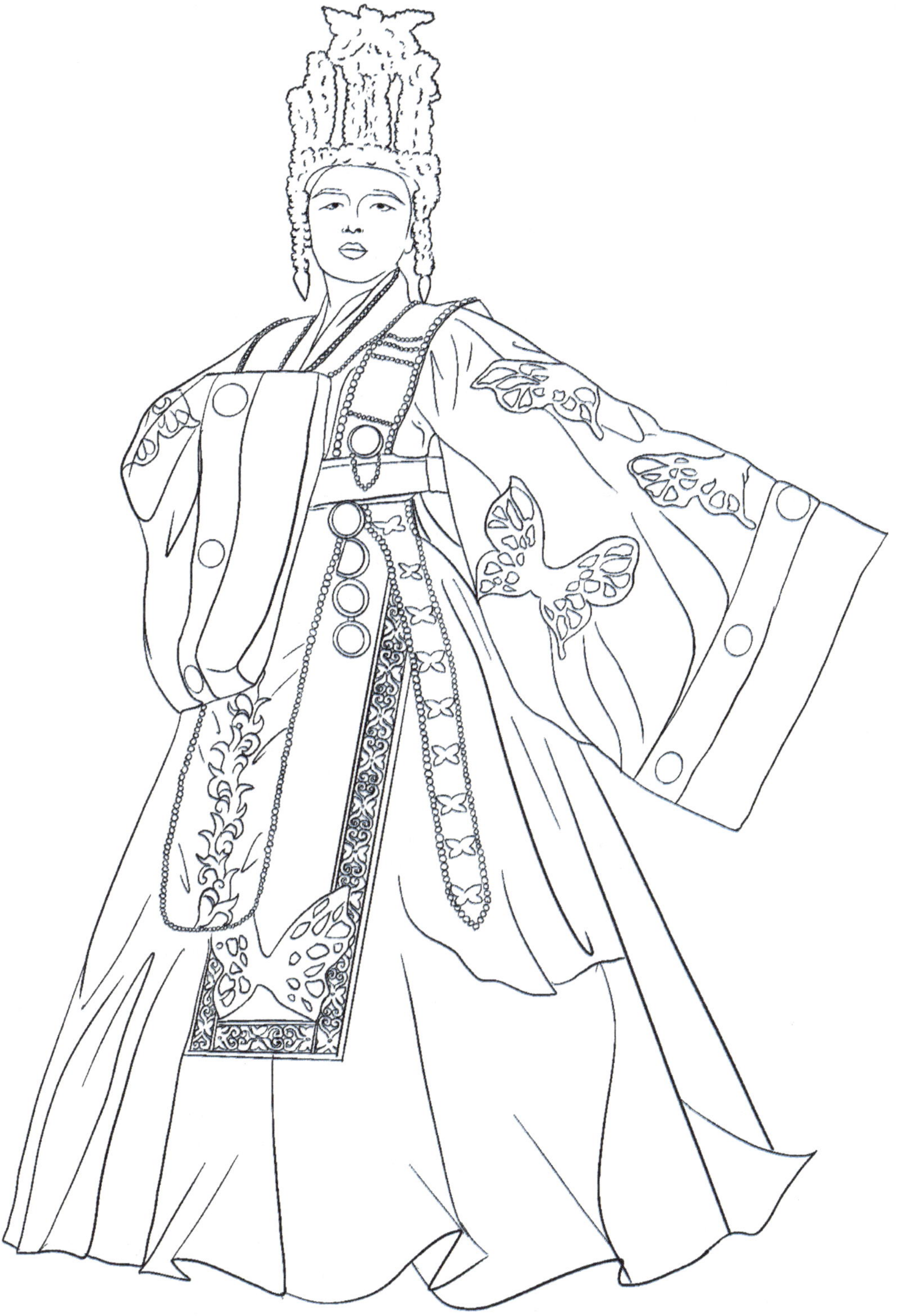

LAOS

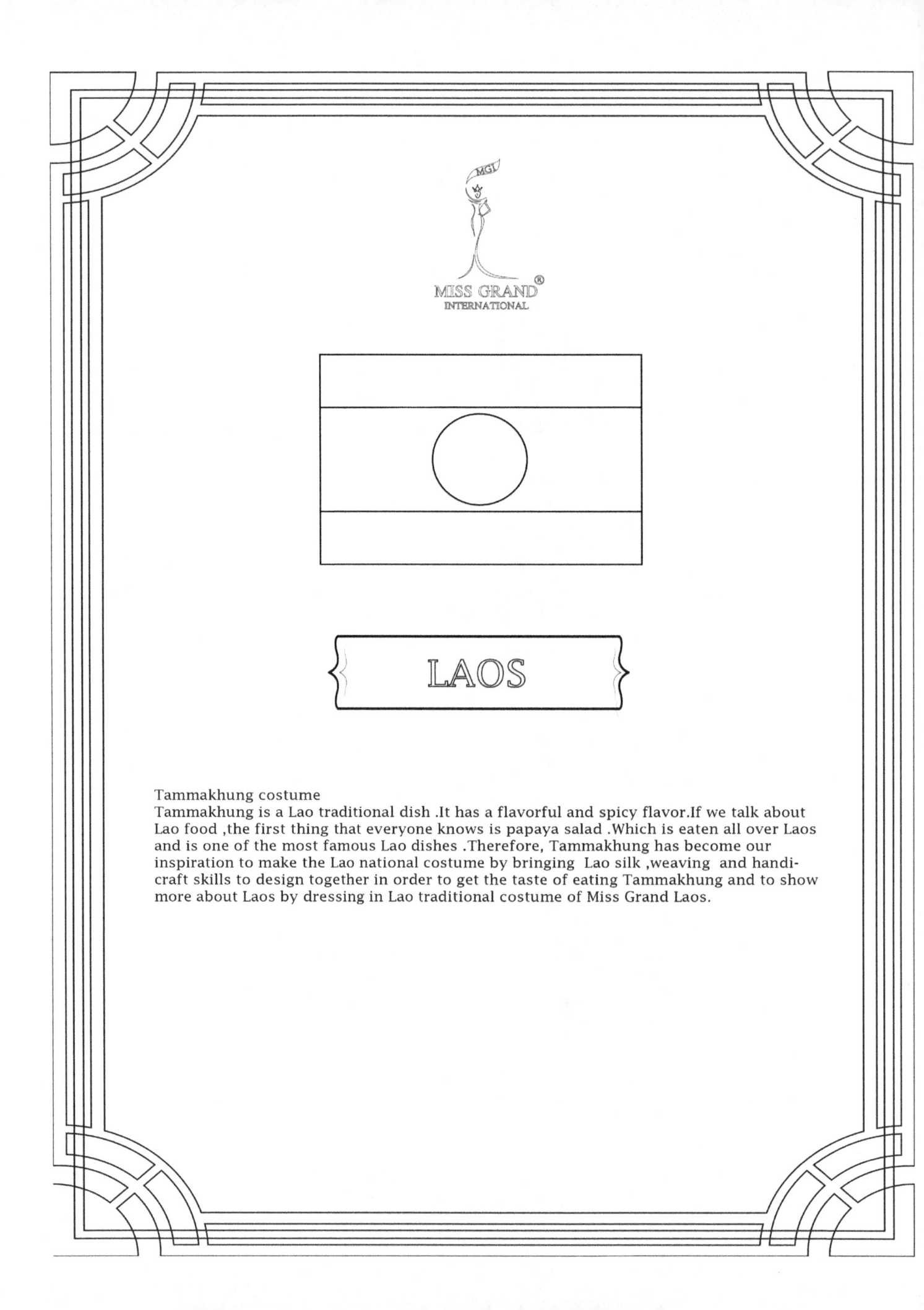

Tammakhung costume
Tammakhung is a Lao traditional dish .It has a flavorful and spicy flavor.If we talk about Lao food ,the first thing that everyone knows is papaya salad .Which is eaten all over Laos and is one of the most famous Lao dishes .Therefore, Tammakhung has become our inspiration to make the Lao national costume by bringing Lao silk ,weaving and handicraft skills to design together in order to get the taste of eating Tammakhung and to show more about Laos by dressing in Lao traditional costume of Miss Grand Laos.

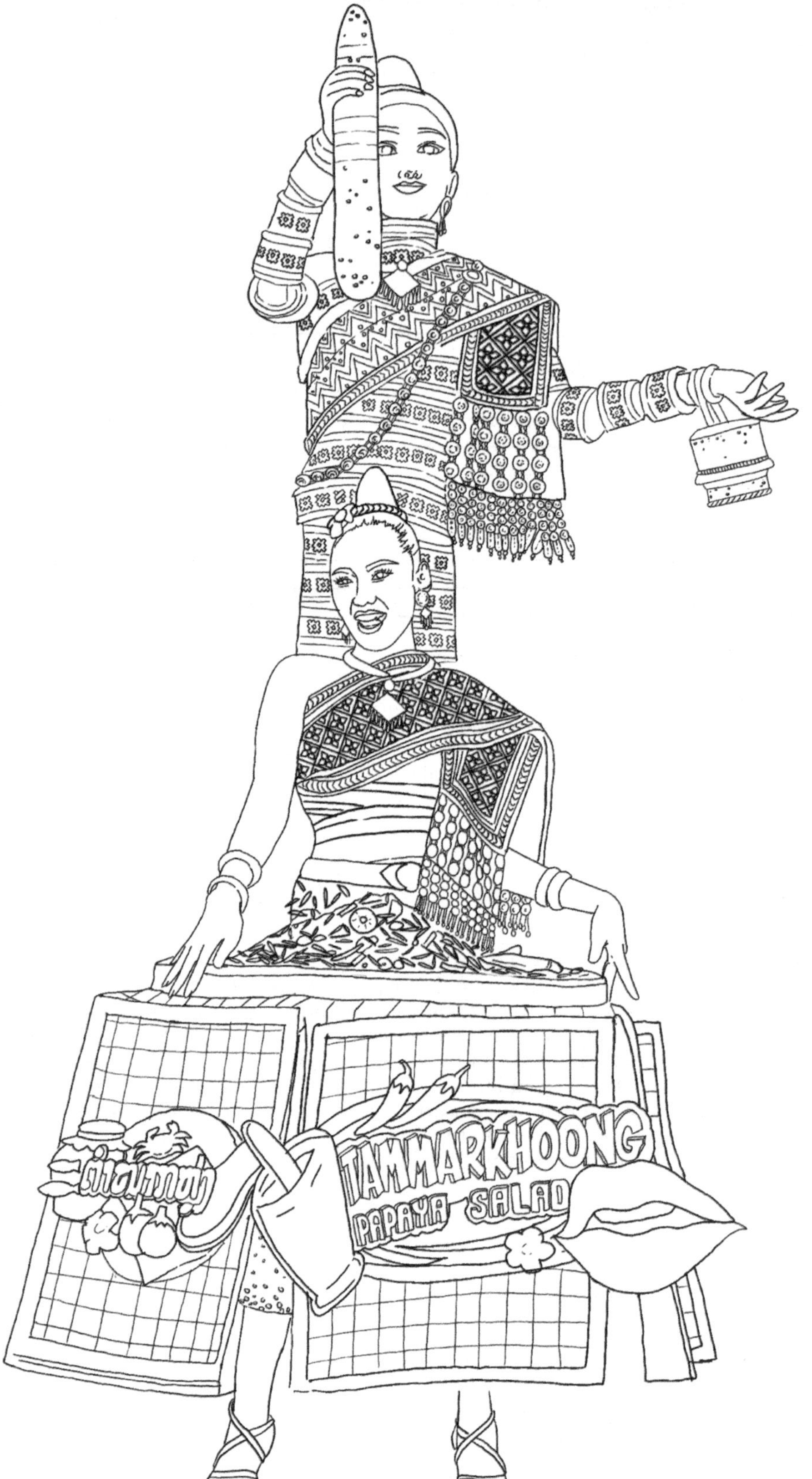
TAMMARKHOONG
PAPAYA SALAD

LIBERIA

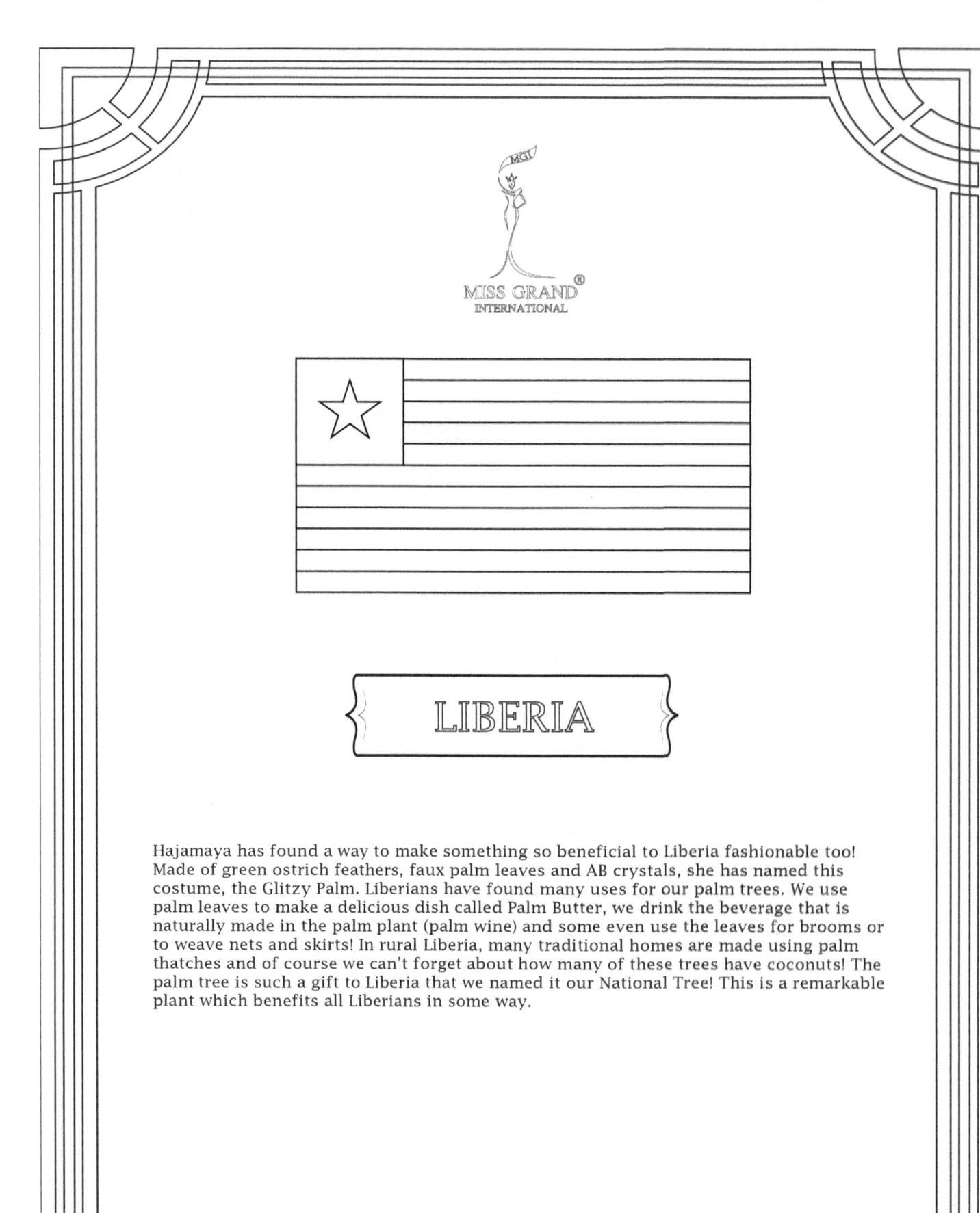

Hajamaya has found a way to make something so beneficial to Liberia fashionable too! Made of green ostrich feathers, faux palm leaves and AB crystals, she has named this costume, the Glitzy Palm. Liberians have found many uses for our palm trees. We use palm leaves to make a delicious dish called Palm Butter, we drink the beverage that is naturally made in the palm plant (palm wine) and some even use the leaves for brooms or to weave nets and skirts! In rural Liberia, many traditional homes are made using palm thatches and of course we can't forget about how many of these trees have coconuts! The palm tree is such a gift to Liberia that we named it our National Tree! This is a remarkable plant which benefits all Liberians in some way.

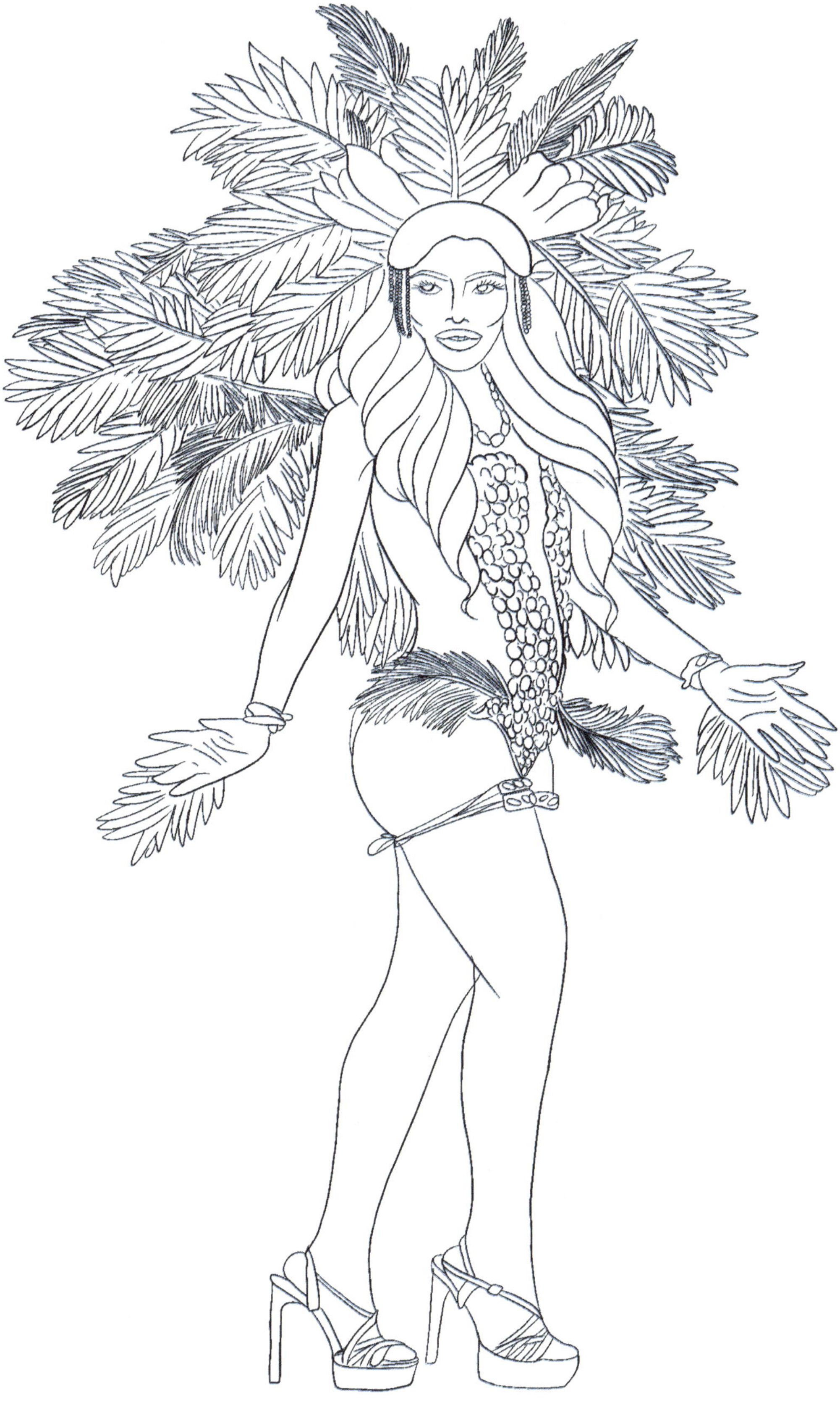

MALAYSIA

Ulek Mayang is one of Malaysia's oldest folk songs and dances originating from the state of Terengganu. In the early days, Ulek Mayang was performed as a healing ritual for fishermen who fall ill at sea and were believed to be caused by sea spirits and could only be cured by calling upon the spirits of the sea and sending them back to the dark watery depths.

The song and performance tells the tale of a sea princess who falls in love with a fisherman while he is at sea. The princess steals the fisherman's soul, causing him to fall into a trance-like state of semi-consciousness. Once they are back on land, the fisherman's friends ask a traditional healer (bomoh) to restore his spirit and bring him back to health.

During the healing ritual, the bomoh summons the spirit of the sea-princess using a mayang (coconut palm blossom), kemenyan (benzoin resin) and offerings of coloured rice., who calls upon her five sisters to help seize the object of her desire. A tug-of-war ensues between the bomoh and the six princesses for the soul of the fishermen. Finally,

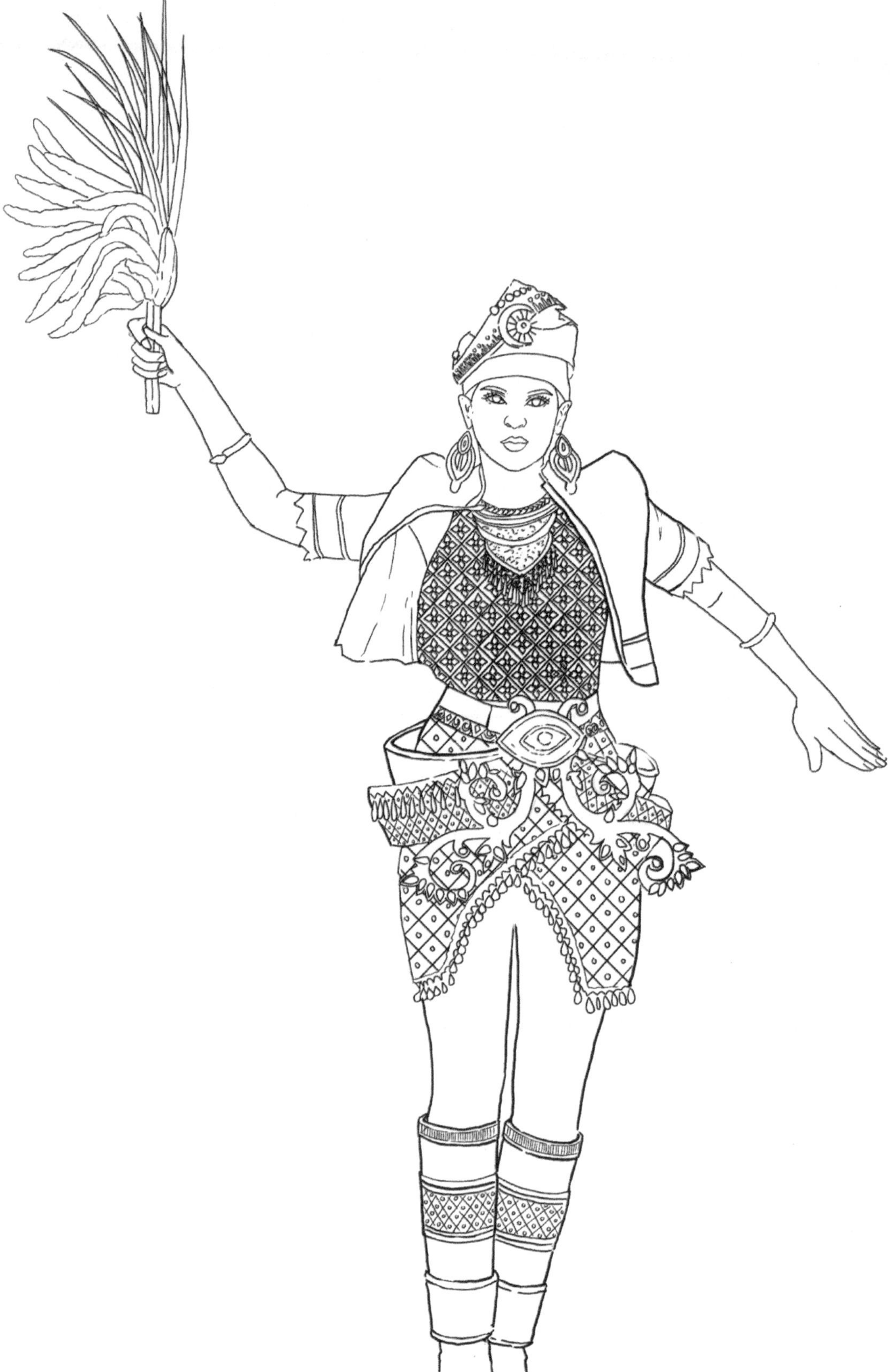

MAURITIUS

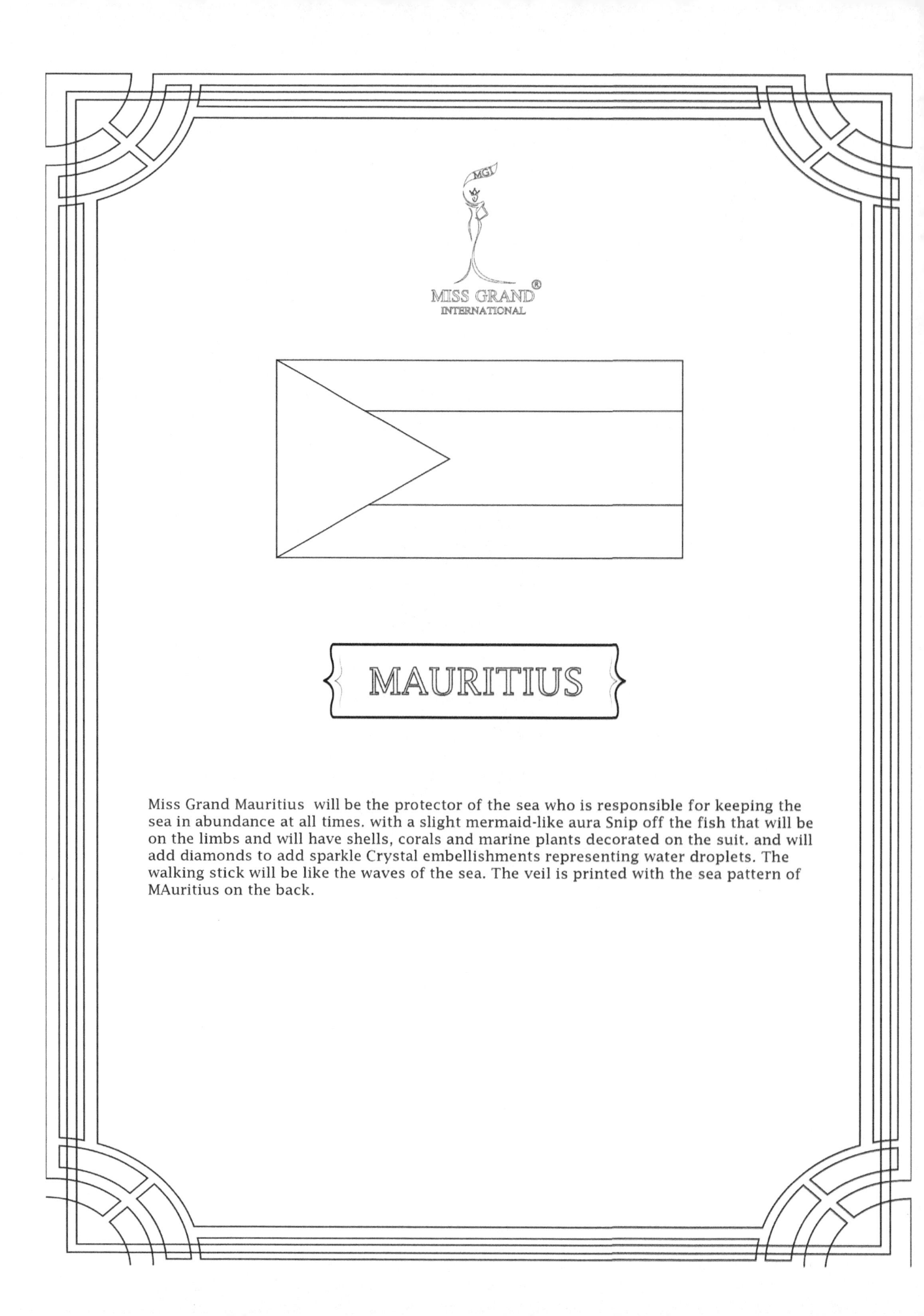

Miss Grand Mauritius will be the protector of the sea who is responsible for keeping the sea in abundance at all times. with a slight mermaid-like aura Snip off the fish that will be on the limbs and will have shells, corals and marine plants decorated on the suit. and will add diamonds to add sparkle Crystal embellishments representing water droplets. The walking stick will be like the waves of the sea. The veil is printed with the sea pattern of MAuritius on the back.

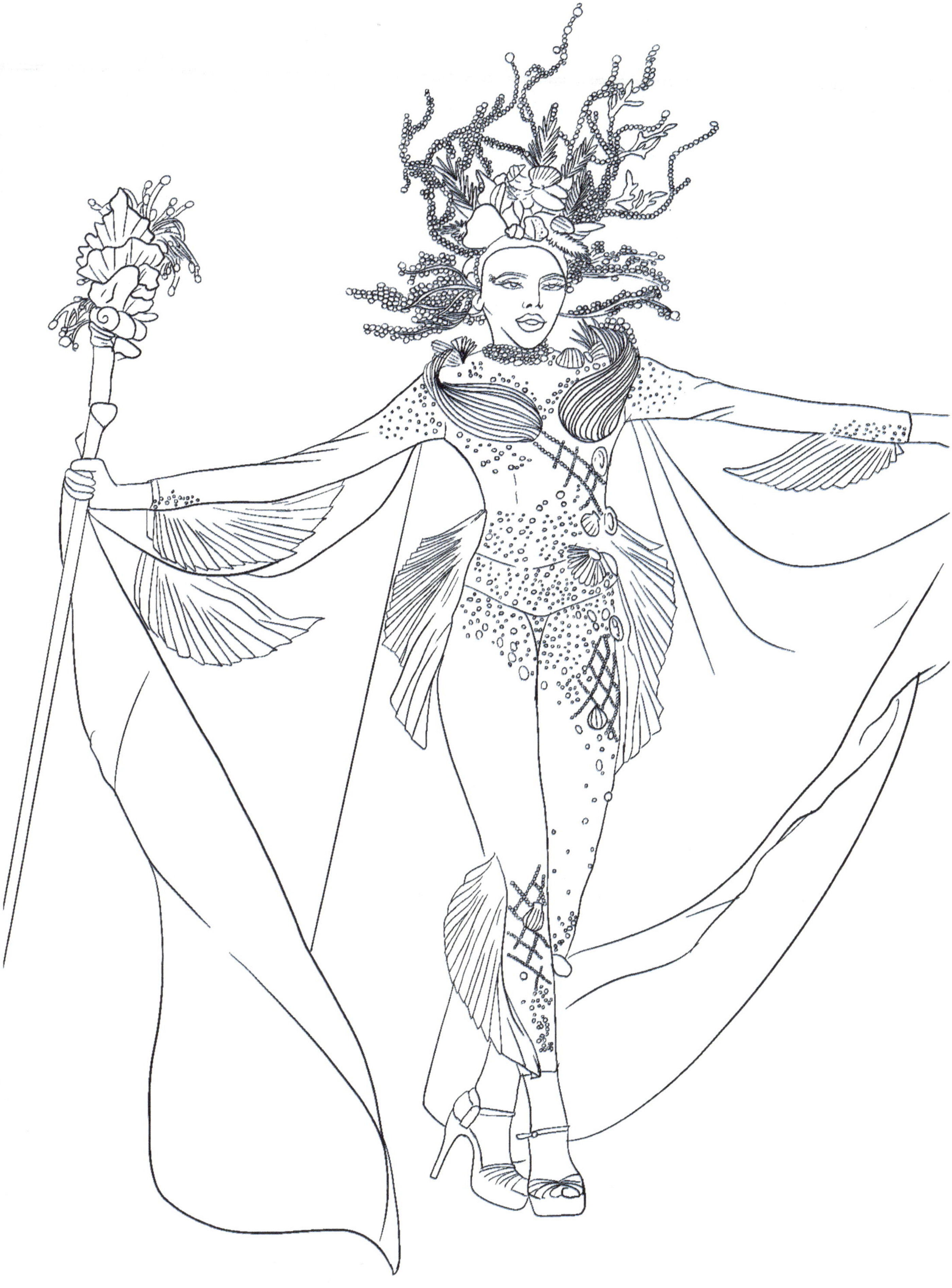

MEXICO

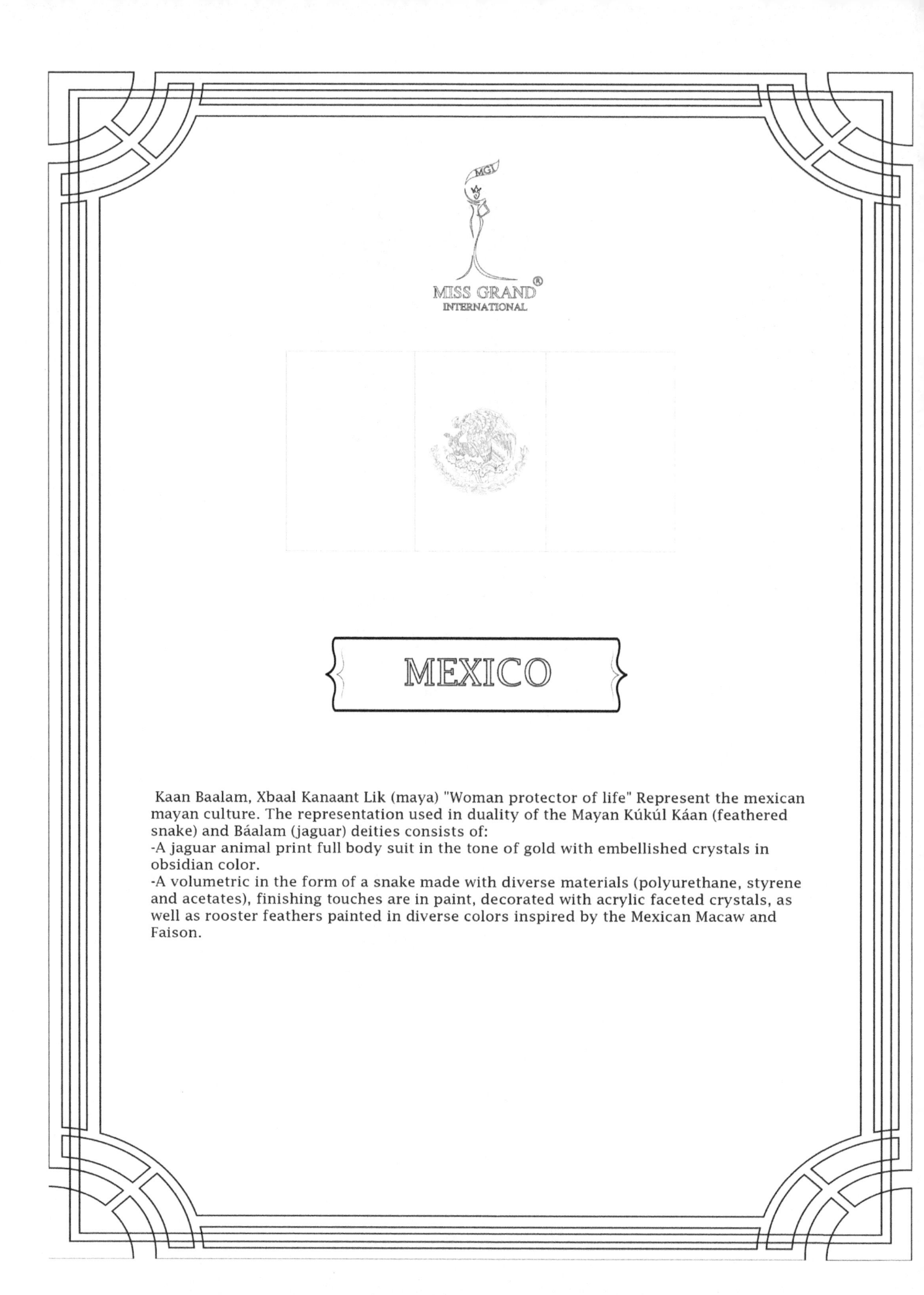

Kaan Baalam, Xbaal Kanaant Lik (maya) "Woman protector of life" Represent the mexican mayan culture. The representation used in duality of the Mayan Kúkúl Káan (feathered snake) and Báalam (jaguar) deities consists of:
-A jaguar animal print full body suit in the tone of gold with embellished crystals in obsidian color.
-A volumetric in the form of a snake made with diverse materials (polyurethane, styrene and acetates), finishing touches are in paint, decorated with acrylic faceted crystals, as well as rooster feathers painted in diverse colors inspired by the Mexican Macaw and Faison.

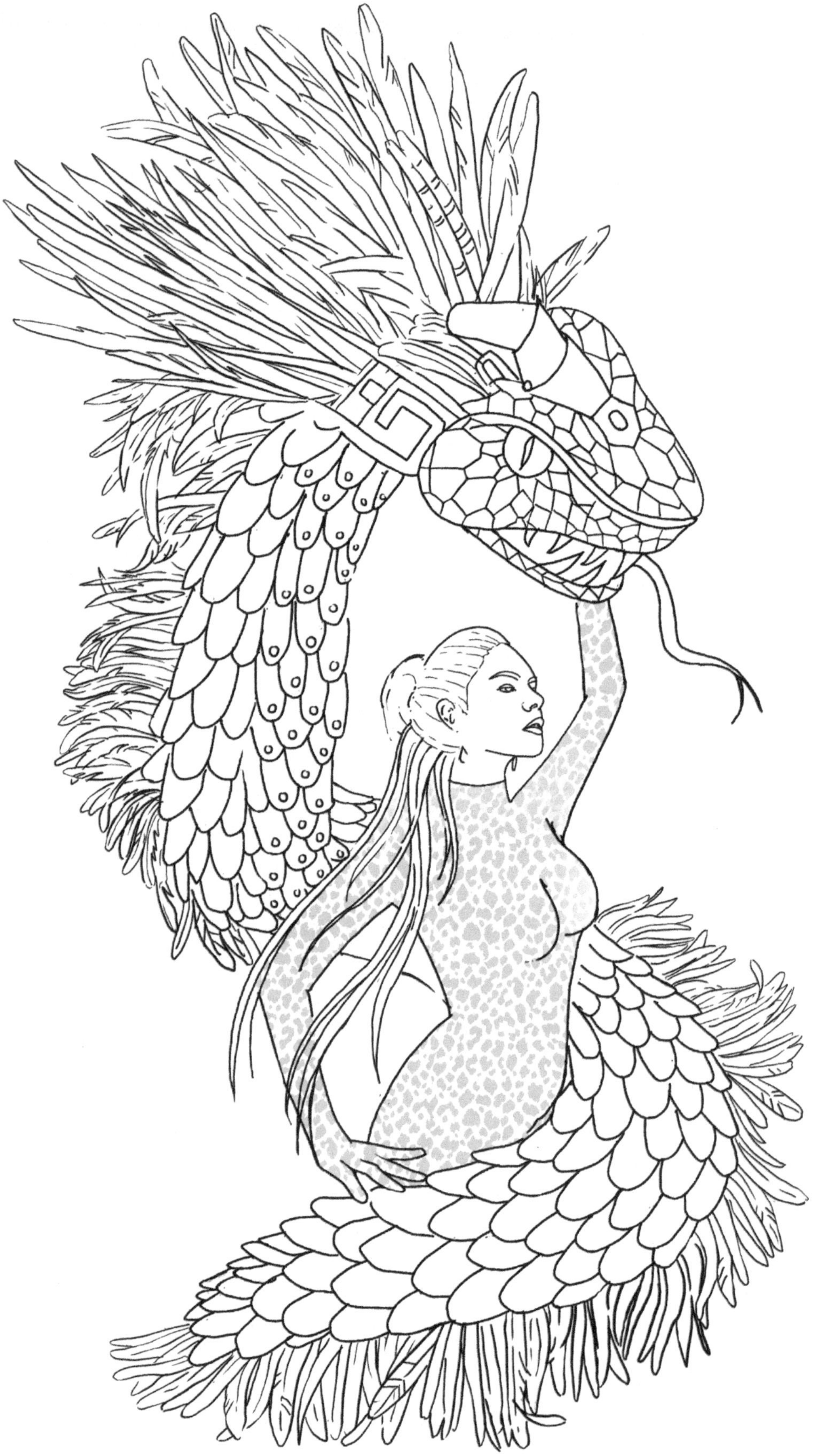

MYANMAR

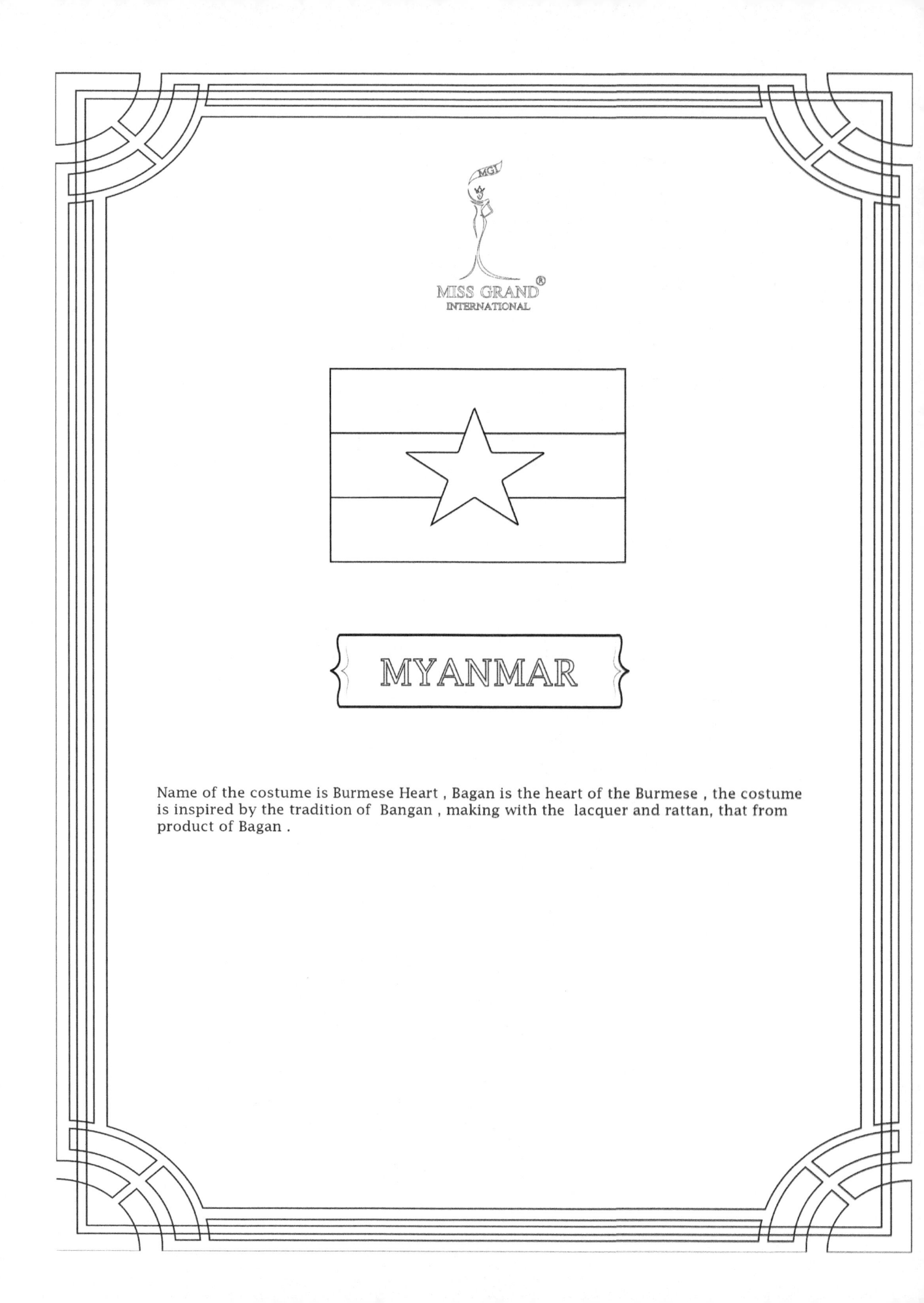

Name of the costume is Burmese Heart , Bagan is the heart of the Burmese , the costume is inspired by the tradition of Bangan , making with the lacquer and rattan, that from product of Bagan .

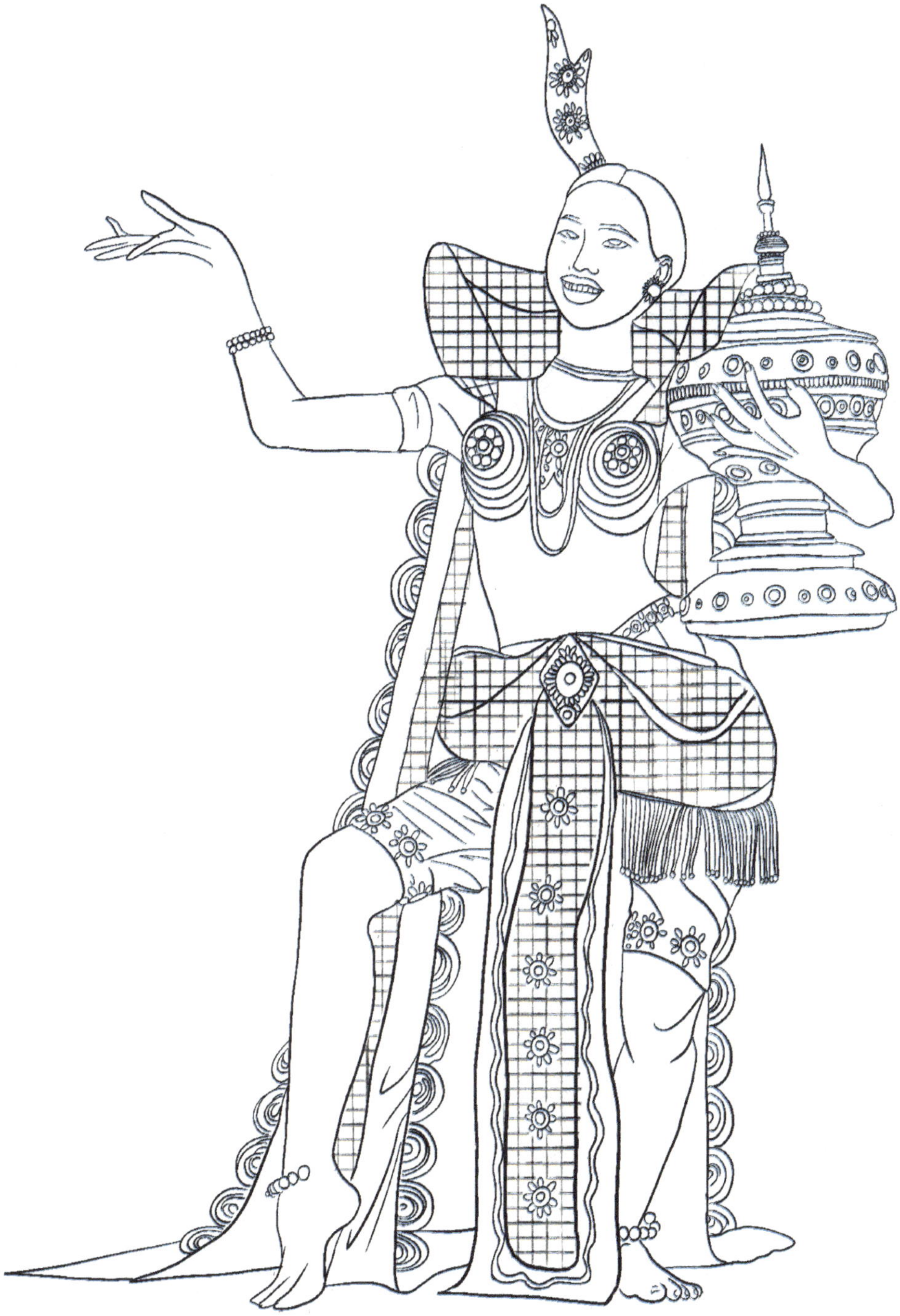

NEPAL

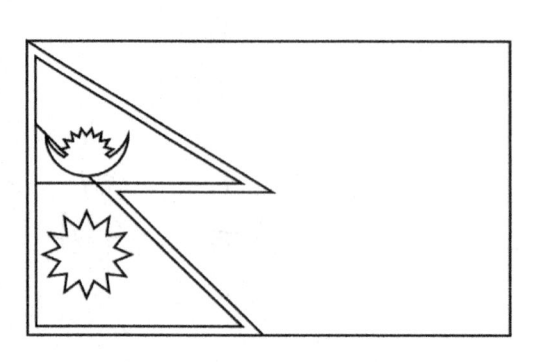

KARUNAMAYA

- God of Compassion is portrayed in this garment, The Special feature of having longest festive time called Jatra in Newari culture, tallest Chariot of 60 feet, worshipped as god of agriculture makes the deity so unique.

- The garment here consists of intricate hand embroidered Skirt and Blouse in red color. The color resembles power, Stability, Security, Action, Courage and emotional survival in the Spiritual realm. Karunamaya being the god who saved people from starvation, drought and blessed with ample crop is denoted by the color red. The hand embroidery consists of Lotus and it's feature which is attributed to the character of compassion.

- The garment is followed by a Chariot at the back. The Green Leaves are Juniper, which is completed using silk tassels carefully handmade and many Symbolic Flags are used in the real Chariot. In the particular design a tapestry known as pataa: is kept as a centre piece.

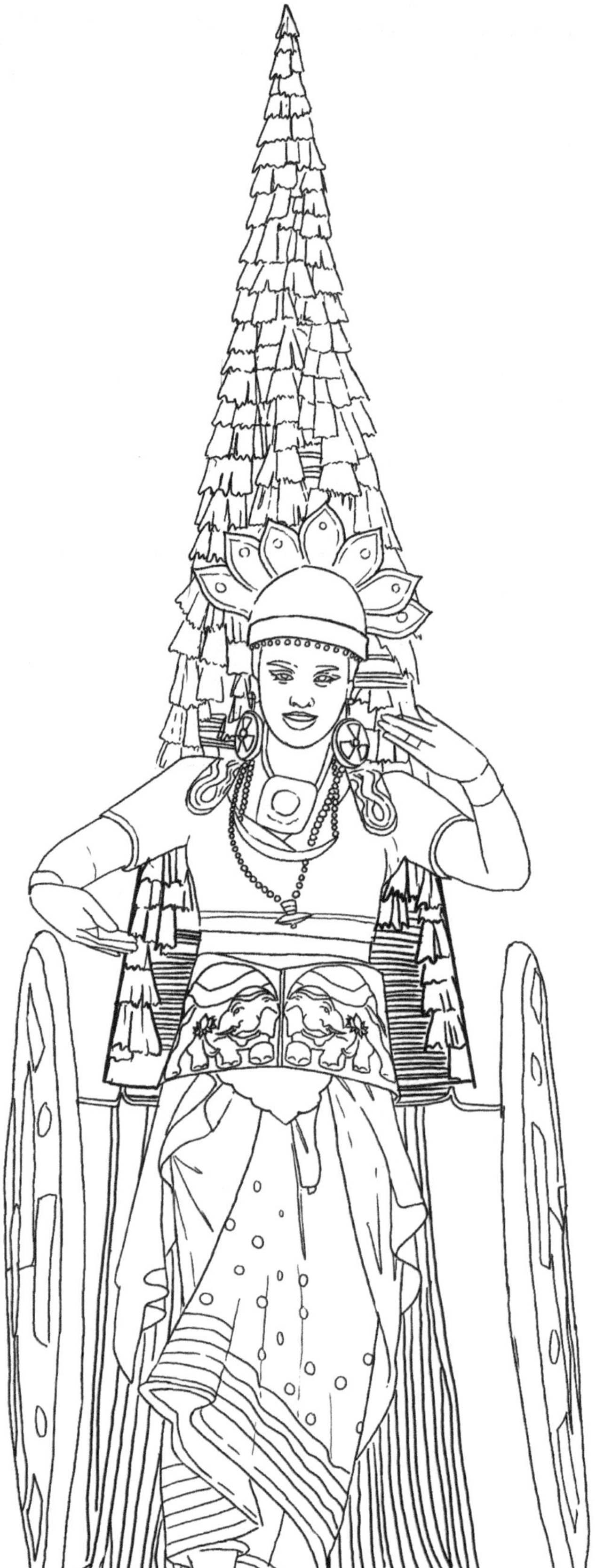

NETHERLANDS

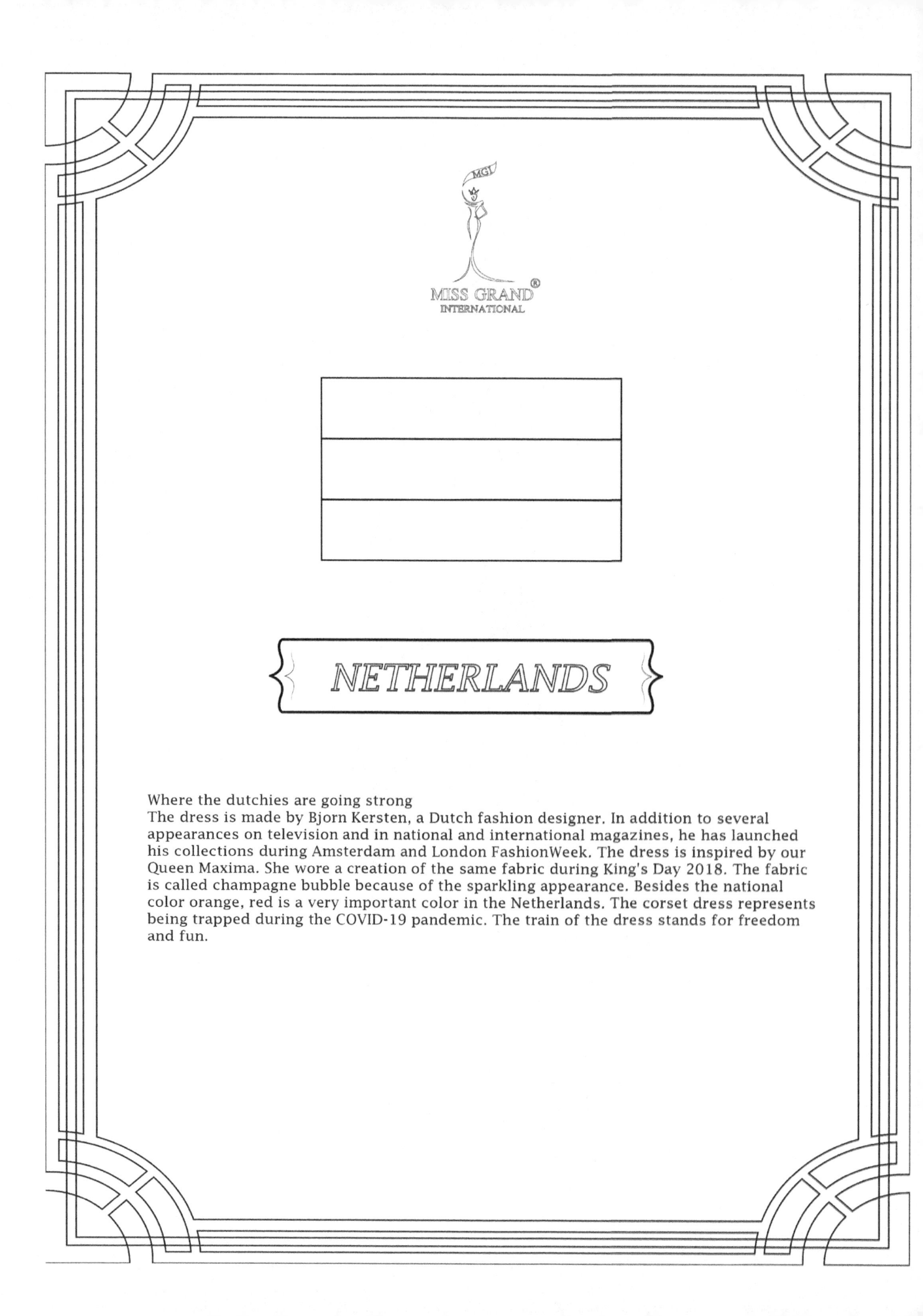

Where the dutchies are going strong
The dress is made by Bjorn Kersten, a Dutch fashion designer. In addition to several appearances on television and in national and international magazines, he has launched his collections during Amsterdam and London FashionWeek. The dress is inspired by our Queen Maxima. She wore a creation of the same fabric during King's Day 2018. The fabric is called champagne bubble because of the sparkling appearance. Besides the national color orange, red is a very important color in the Netherlands. The corset dress represents being trapped during the COVID-19 pandemic. The train of the dress stands for freedom and fun.

NICARAGUA

XILONEN, PROTECTOR OF CORN!
With the history in the body and an aesthetic base that adduces to our pre-Hispanic era, this scenic development of costumes arises.
This design features our Pre-Hispanic woman Xilonen, a woman with a strong character who was always facing new challenges and obstacles, charismatic by nature and those around her, feeling deep affection and admiration for her.
Aesthetically, this pre-Hispanic clothing highlights the value of the cultivation of corn, one of the main economic and gastronomic items of our land. The painting, the petroglyphs engraved on our stones were one of the main ways of creating history that our ancestors had, therefore they become one of our most valuable artistic heritages that could be inherited from us, not only because of their undeniable aesthetic quality but also because of their value. tangible that they represent, in them remain cultural traits and histories of our country.

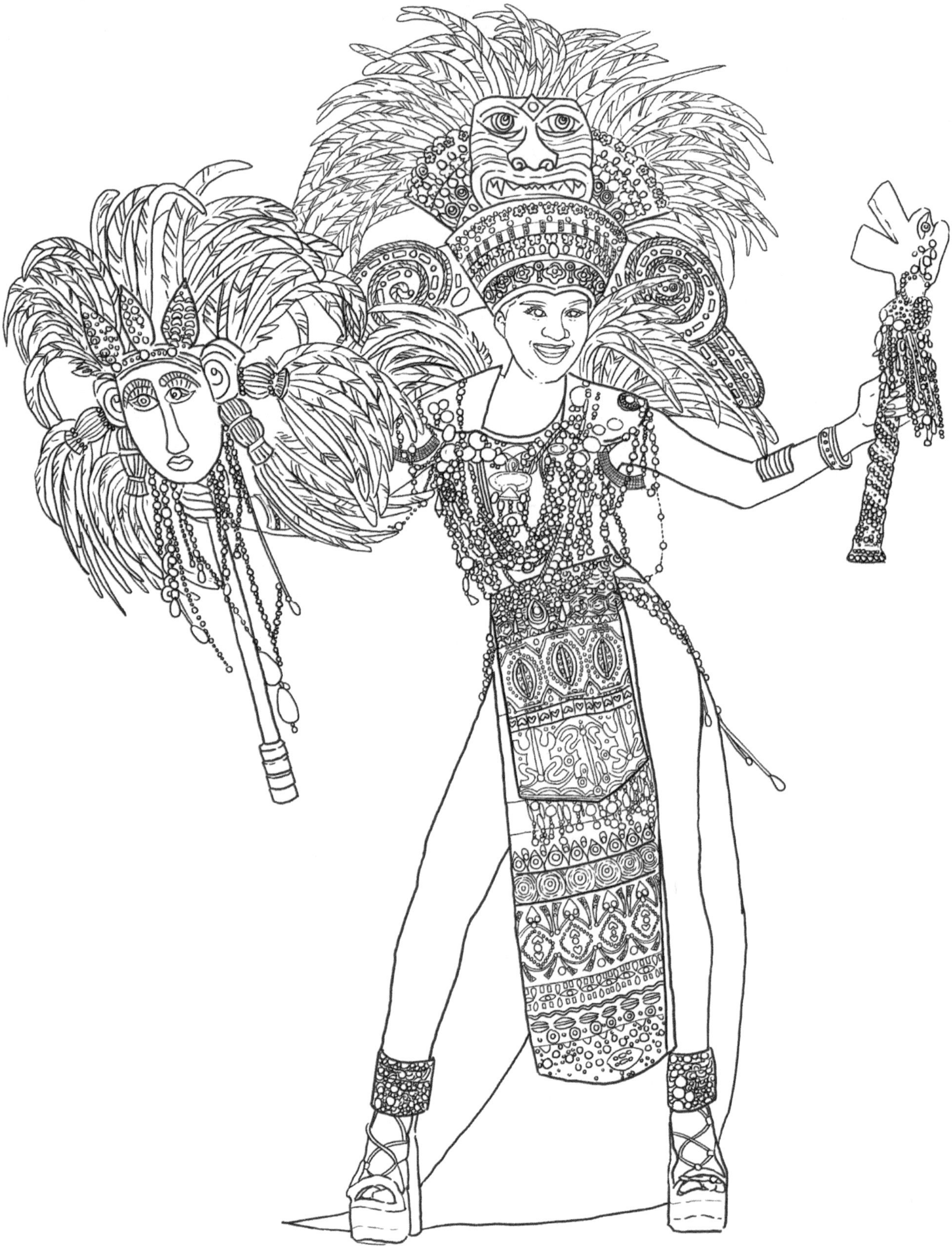

NIGERIA

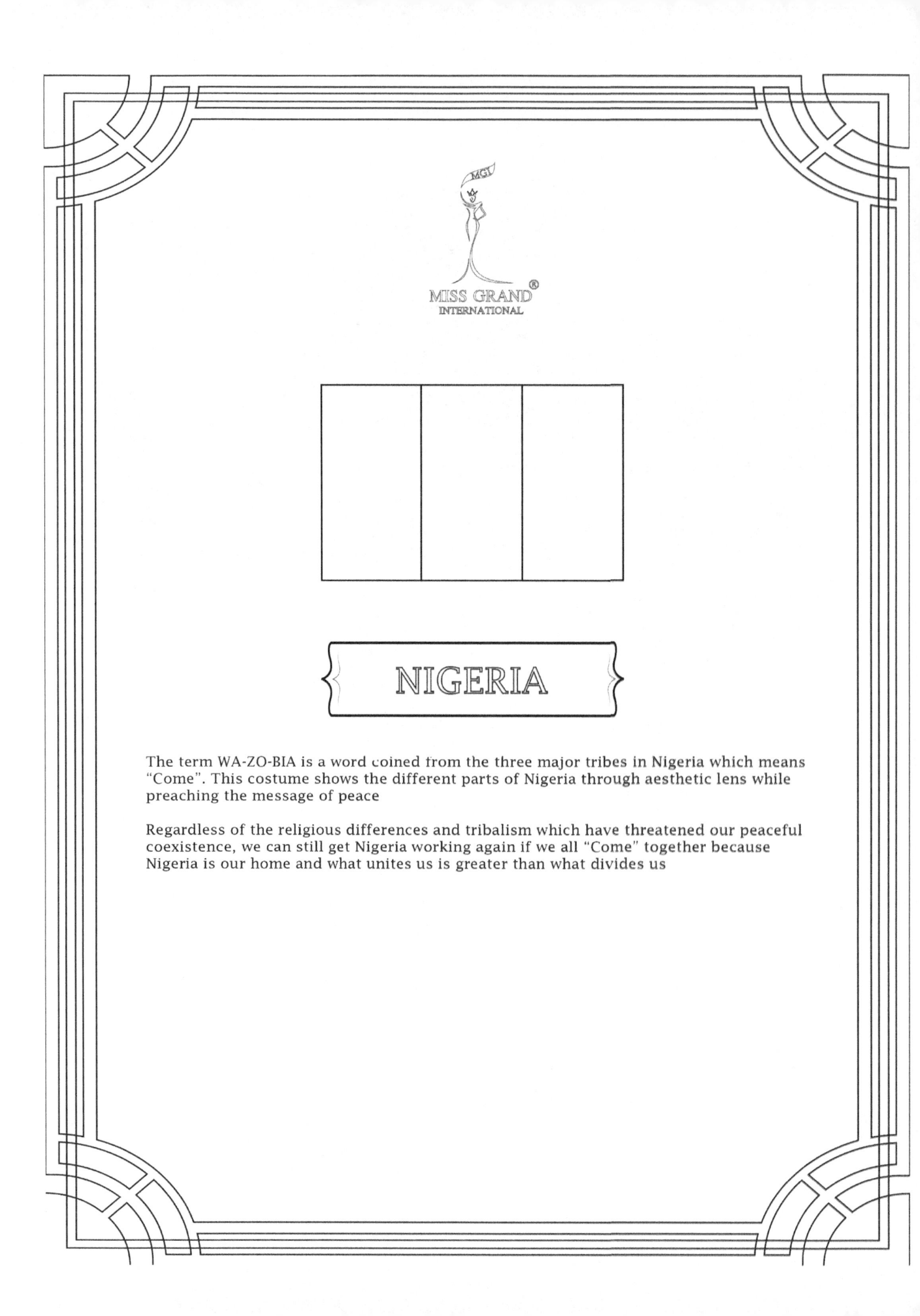

The term WA-ZO-BIA is a word coined from the three major tribes in Nigeria which means "Come". This costume shows the different parts of Nigeria through aesthetic lens while preaching the message of peace

Regardless of the religious differences and tribalism which have threatened our peaceful coexistence, we can still get Nigeria working again if we all "Come" together because Nigeria is our home and what unites us is greater than what divides us

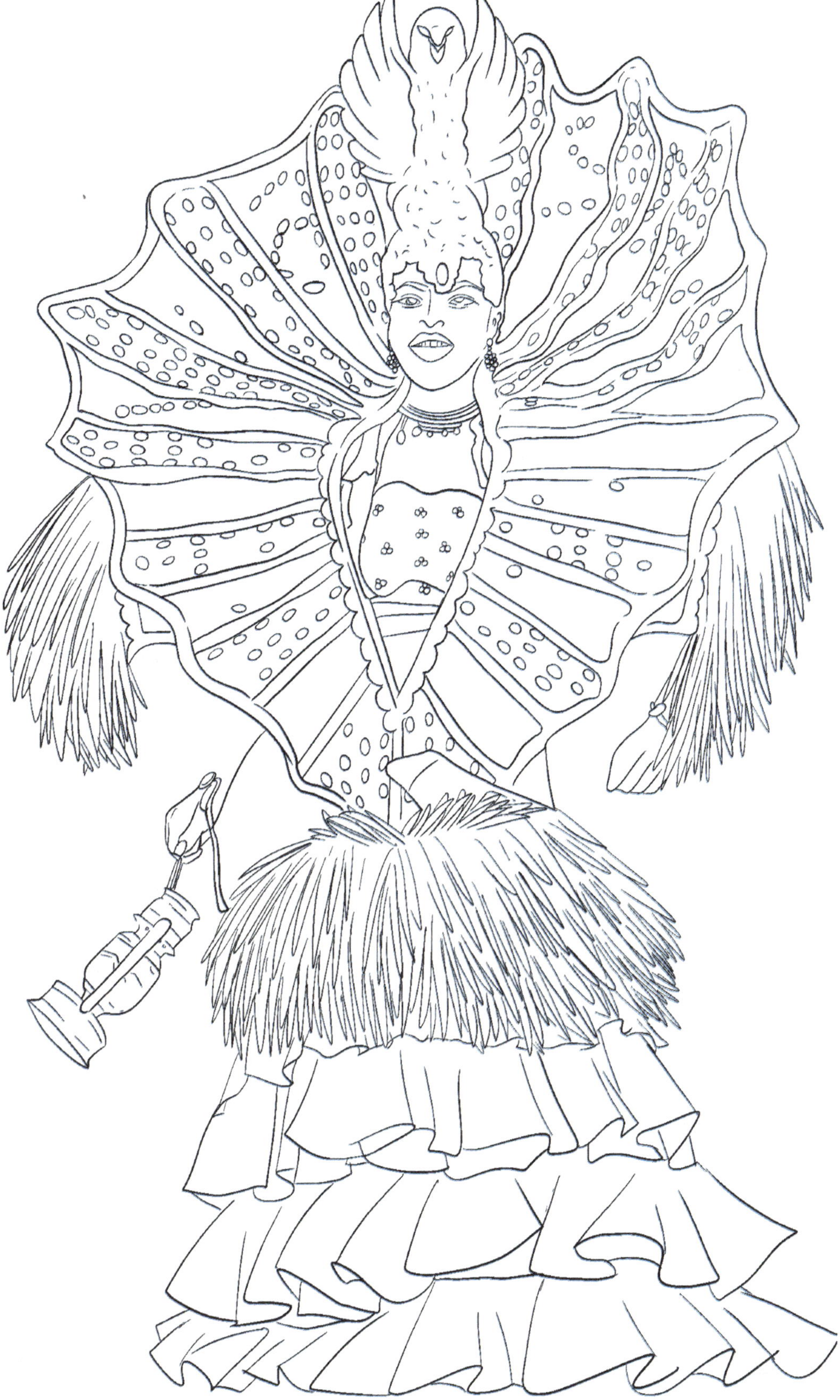

NORTHERN IRELAND

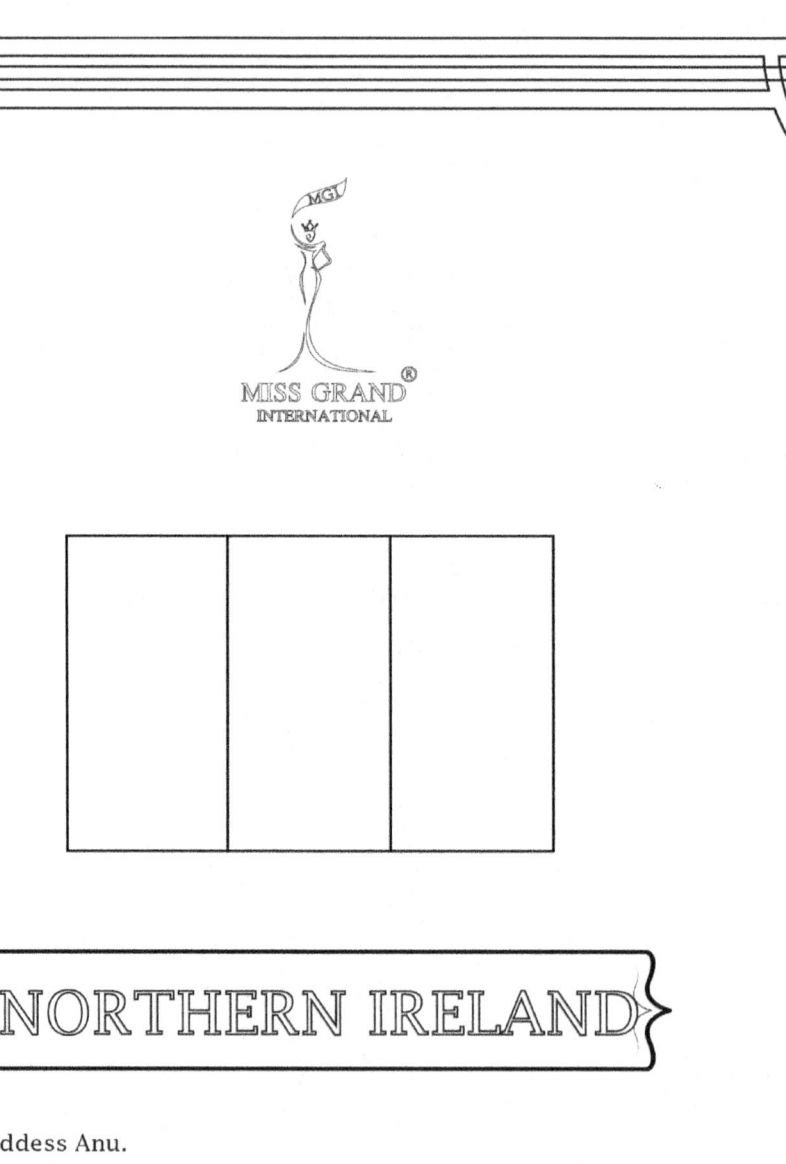

The Irish Earth Goddess Anu.

In Irish Folklore, Anu was the beautiful queen of nature, from whom all life emerged. She embodied the earth, rivers, and the sea. She offered beauty, abundance, regeneration and nurturing.

In ancient times, the Celts worshipped, and considered Anu to be the mother of all Celtic gods. Her most powerful gift was bountiful harvest in the darkest days.

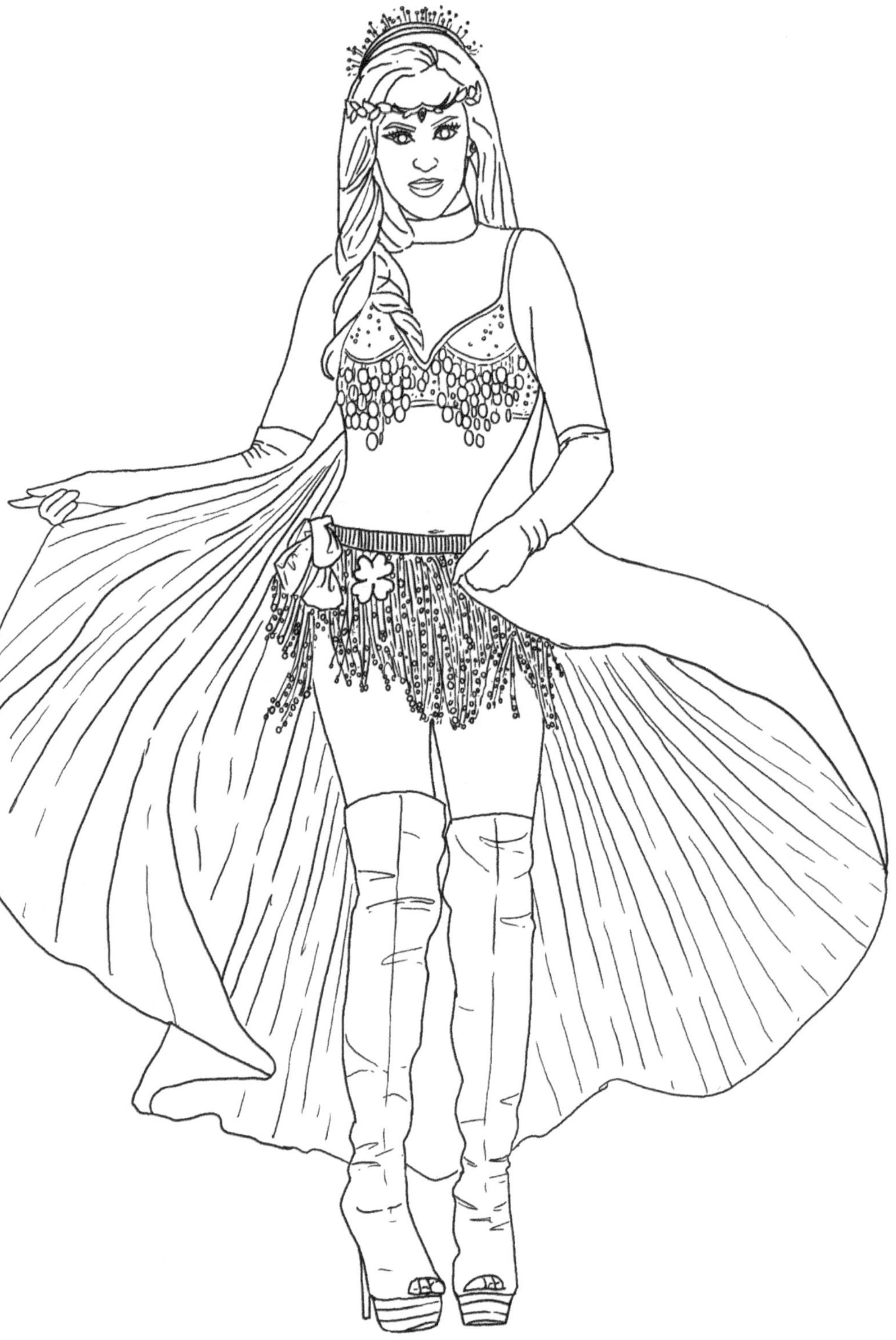

PAKISTAN

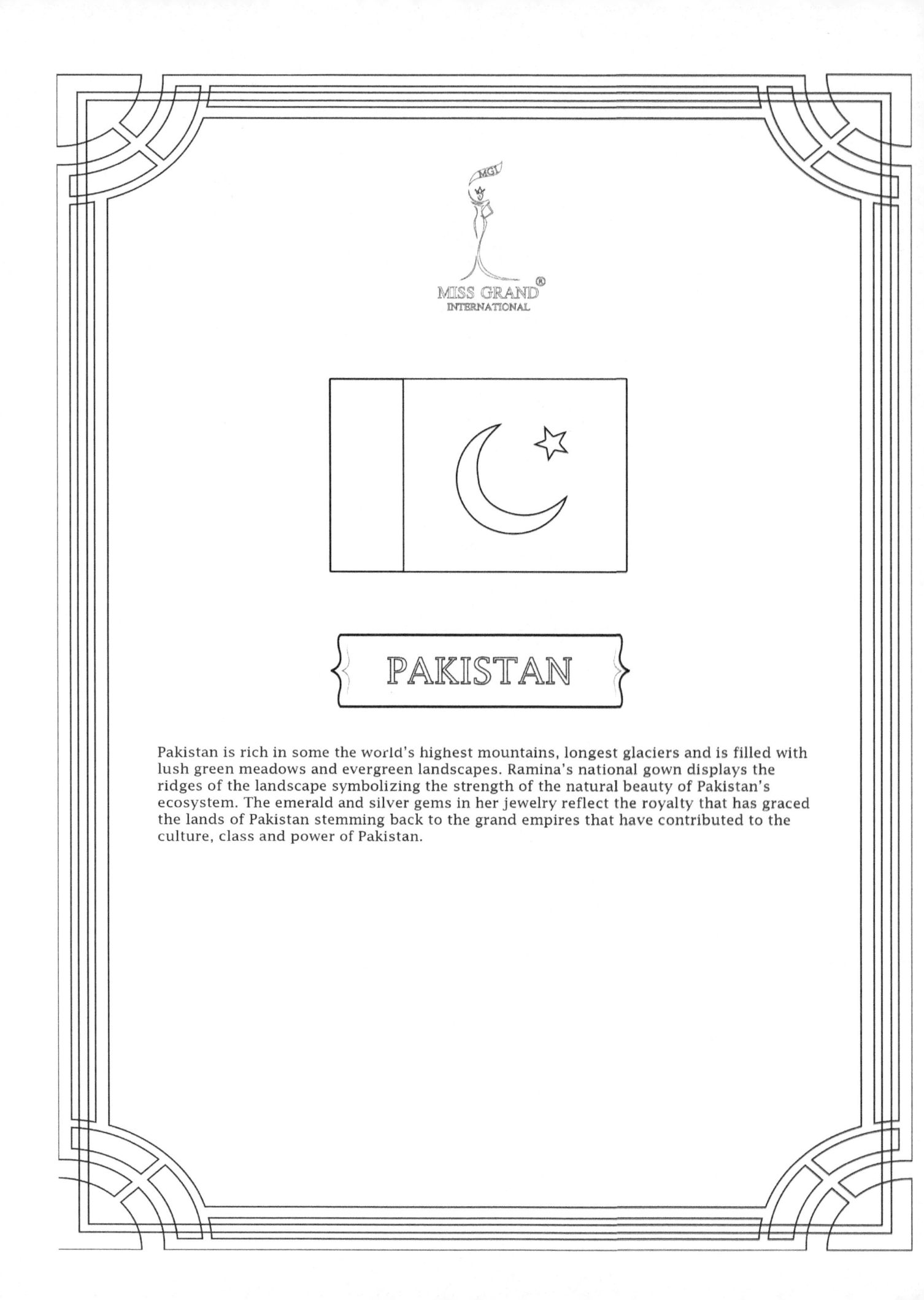

Pakistan is rich in some the world's highest mountains, longest glaciers and is filled with lush green meadows and evergreen landscapes. Ramina's national gown displays the ridges of the landscape symbolizing the strength of the natural beauty of Pakistan's ecosystem. The emerald and silver gems in her jewelry reflect the royalty that has graced the lands of Pakistan stemming back to the grand empires that have contributed to the culture, class and power of Pakistan.

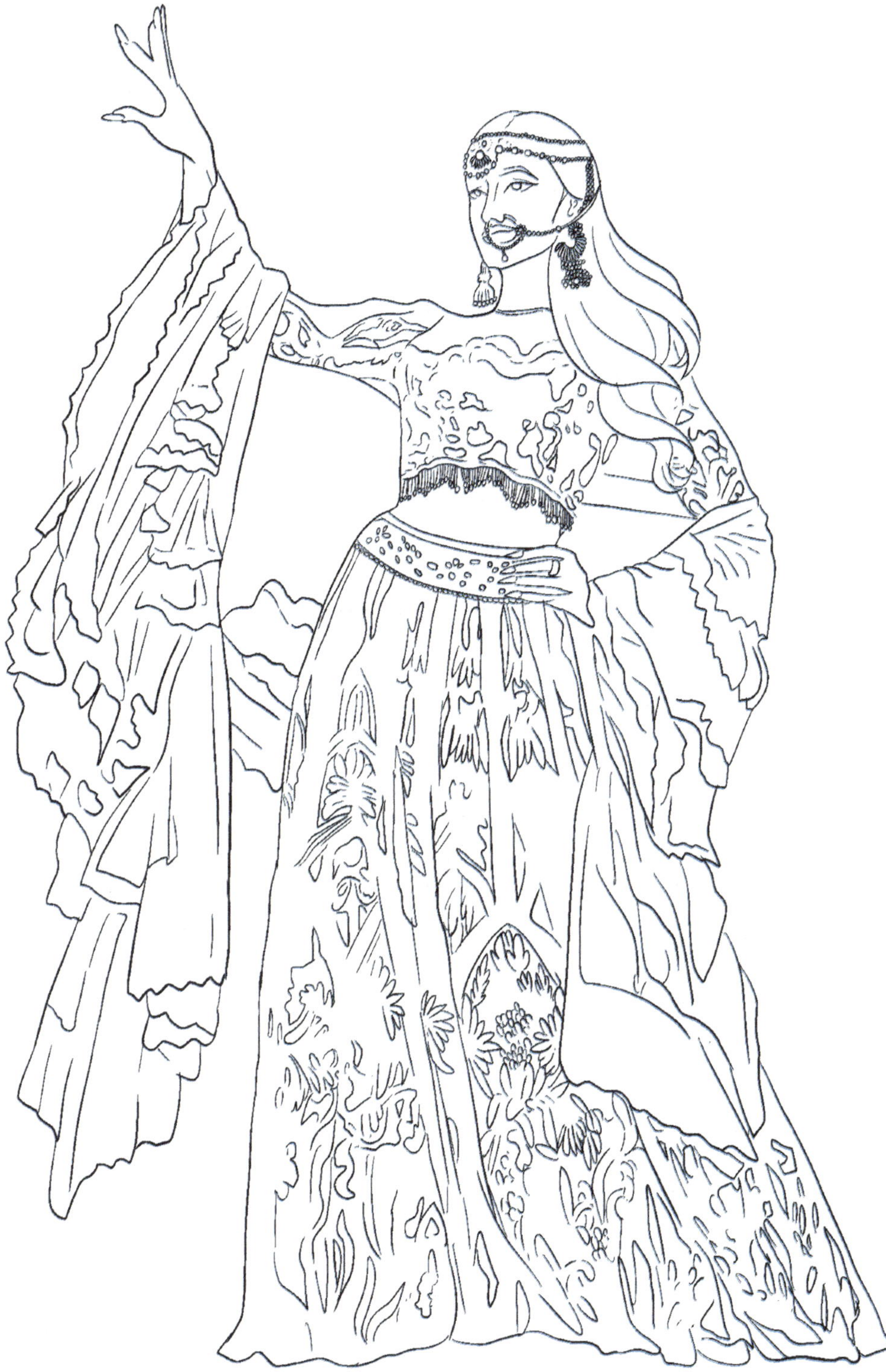

PANAMA

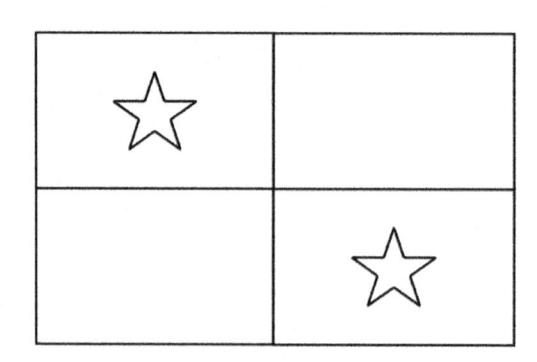

In an archaeological site in the province of cocle in the republic of panama, near the bay of parita. It can be described as a necropolis and a "paradigm of a hierarchical society of headship". Based on the dates of gold and ceramic works found at the site, it has remained intact since the last excavations in 1940, its mortuary ruins are considered a critical resource for archaeologists since they contribute to the interpretation of the social dynamics of the region among the 500 - 1500 AD Little is known about the Conte site and the individuals that reside there, which makes it more mysterious and interesting. Several theories have been formulated about the site, some of which consider the site "summer residence" or common cemetery. Those buried in the tombs have been identified as both "noble families" as well as "chiefs and warriors fallen in battle." Archaeologists are fairly certain of the dates of use of the site. These have been established by the dating of the gold and ceramic work found in the tombs. From these artifacts it is revealed that the site was used from about 450 AD. until the year 900

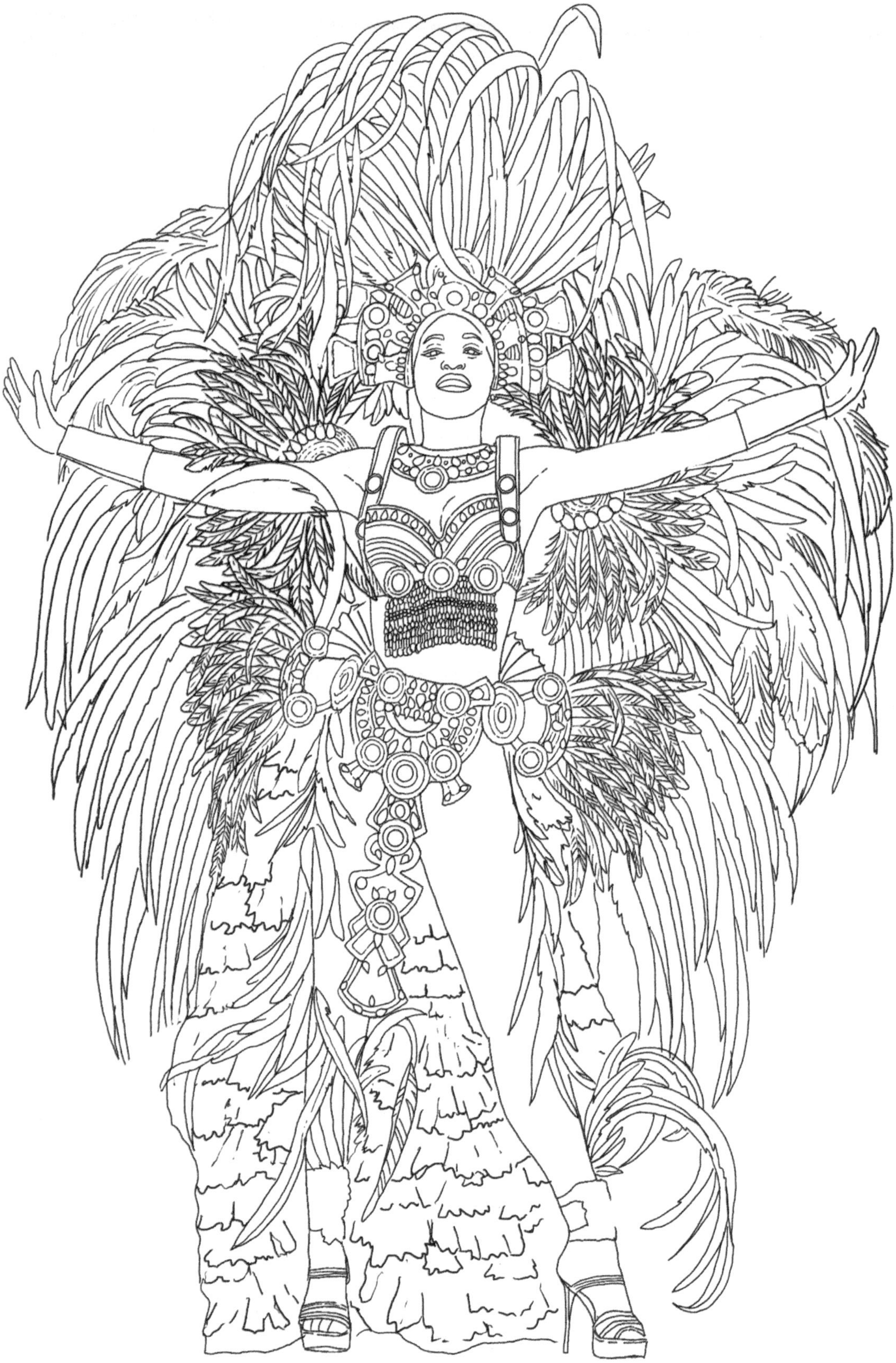

PARAGUAY

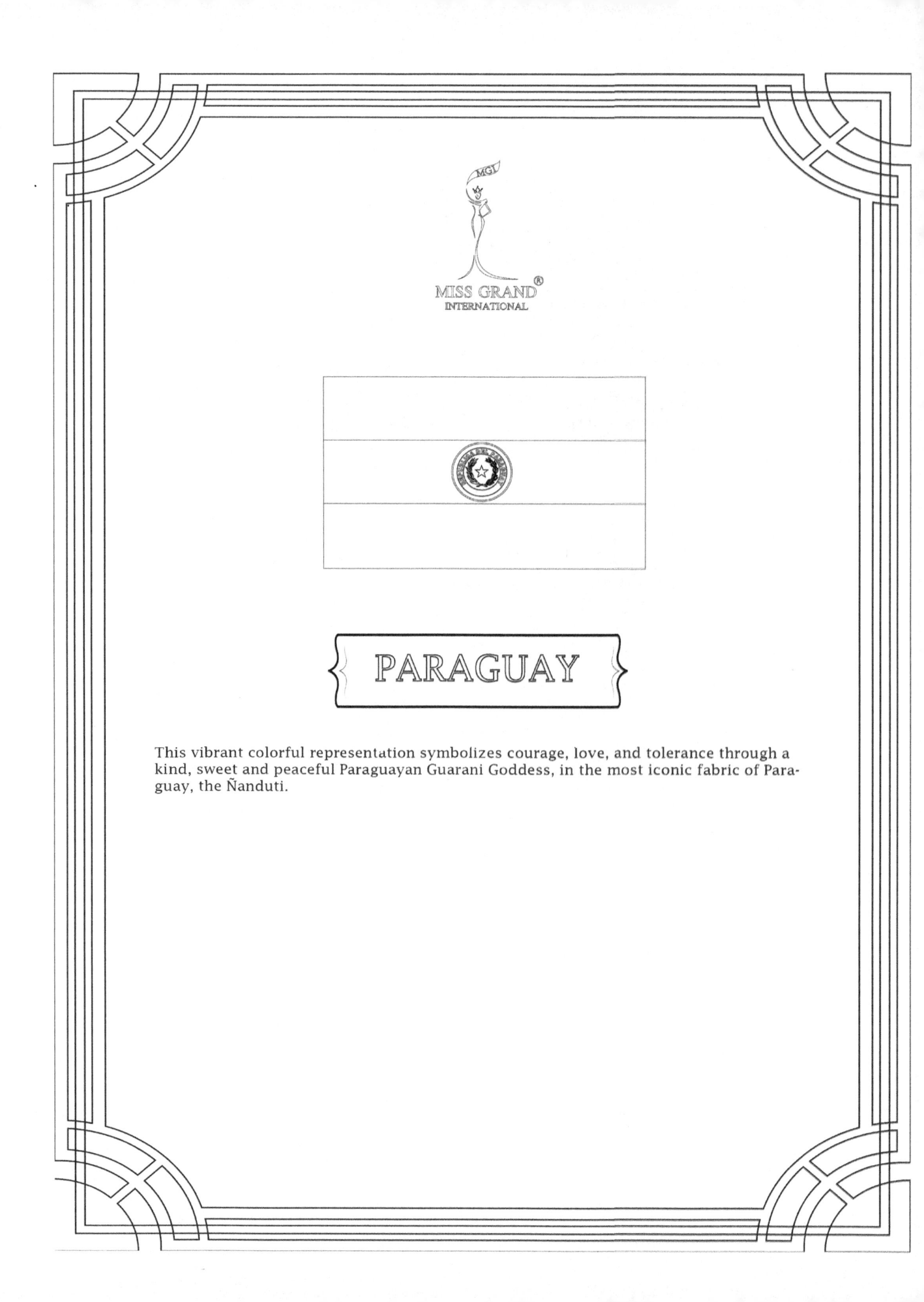

This vibrant colorful representation symbolizes courage, love, and tolerance through a kind, sweet and peaceful Paraguayan Guarani Goddess, in the most iconic fabric of Paraguay, the Ñanduti.

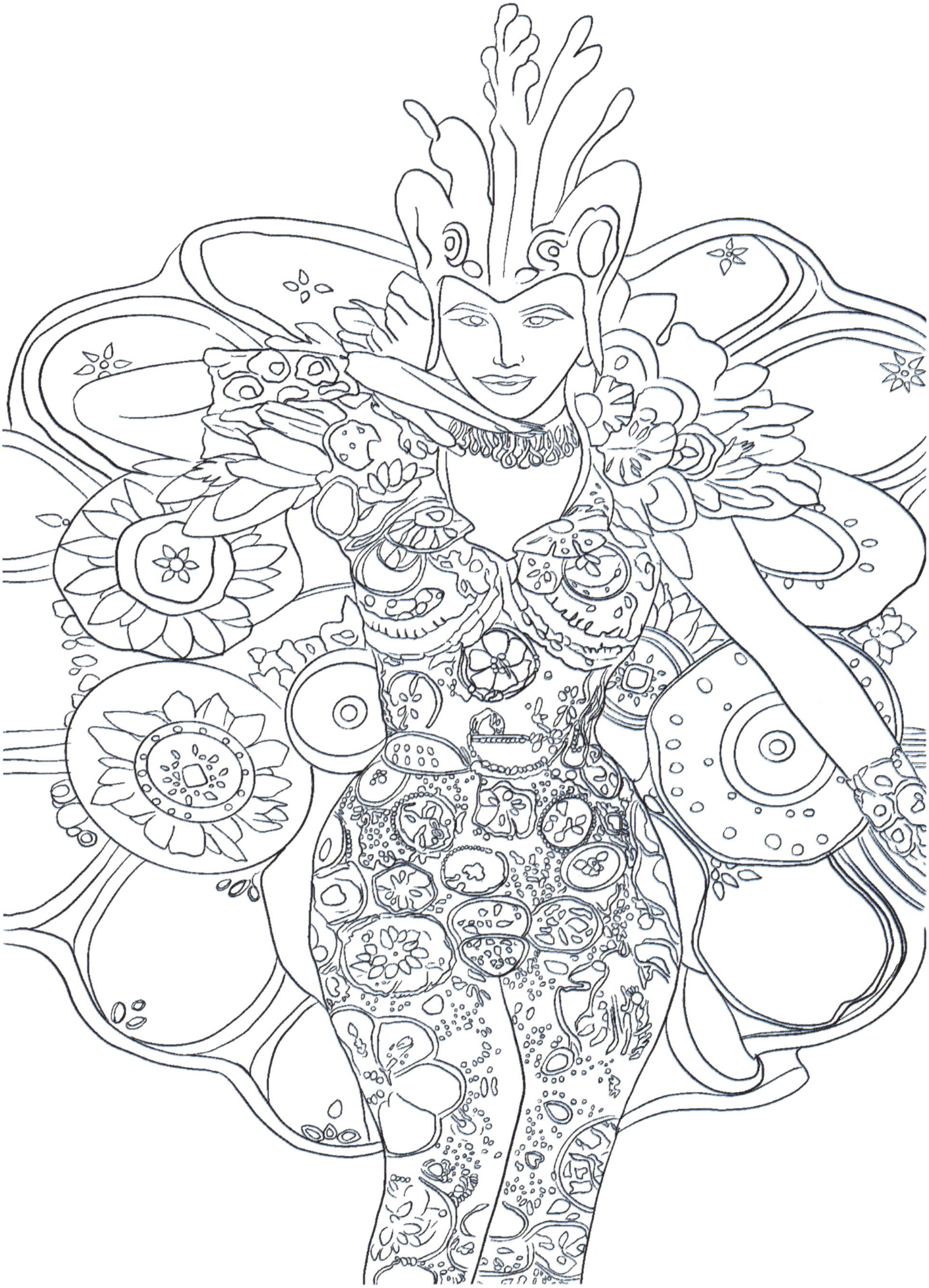

PERU

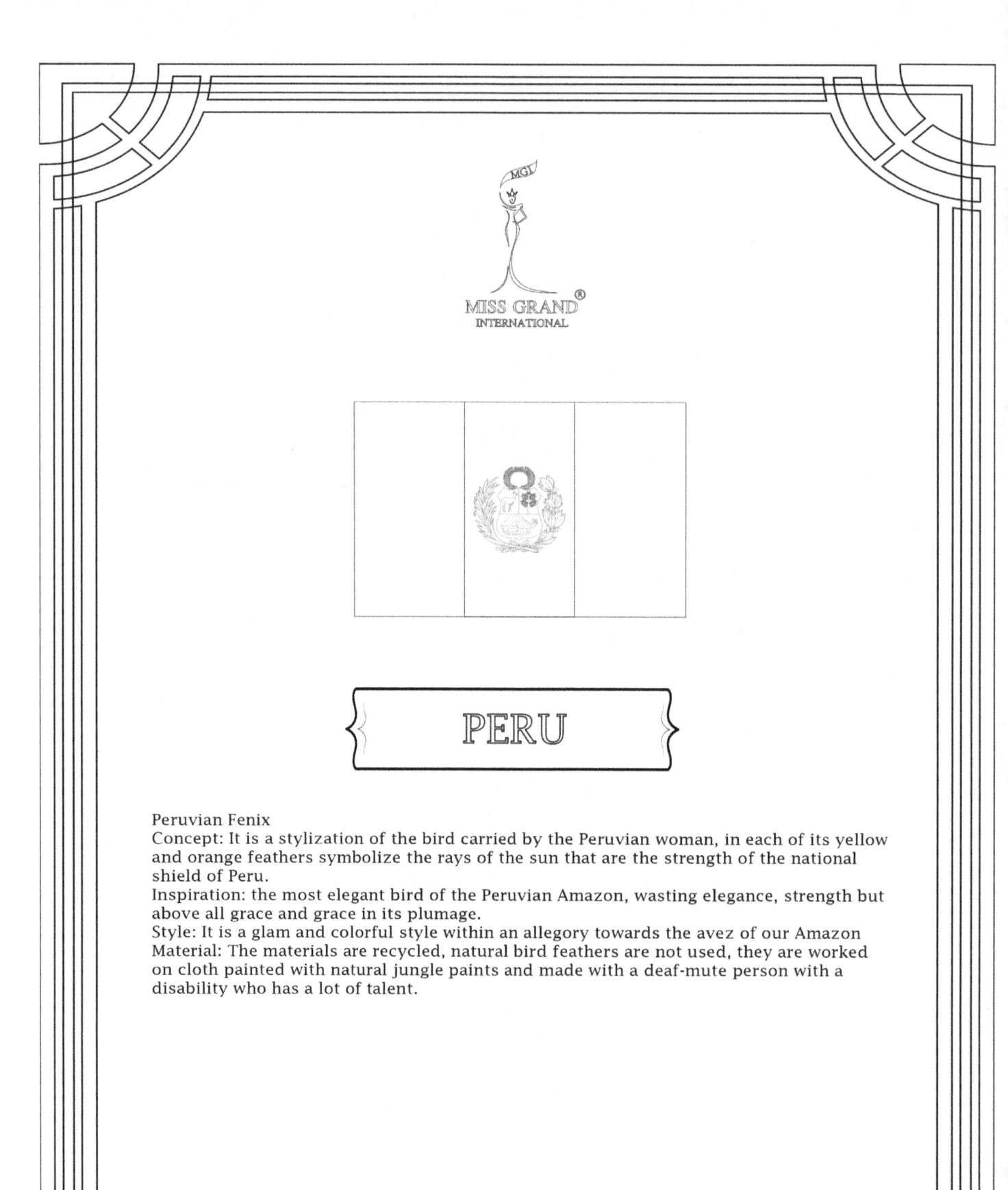

Peruvian Fenix
Concept: It is a stylization of the bird carried by the Peruvian woman, in each of its yellow and orange feathers symbolize the rays of the sun that are the strength of the national shield of Peru.
Inspiration: the most elegant bird of the Peruvian Amazon, wasting elegance, strength but above all grace and grace in its plumage.
Style: It is a glam and colorful style within an allegory towards the avez of our Amazon
Material: The materials are recycled, natural bird feathers are not used, they are worked on cloth painted with natural jungle paints and made with a deaf-mute person with a disability who has a lot of talent.

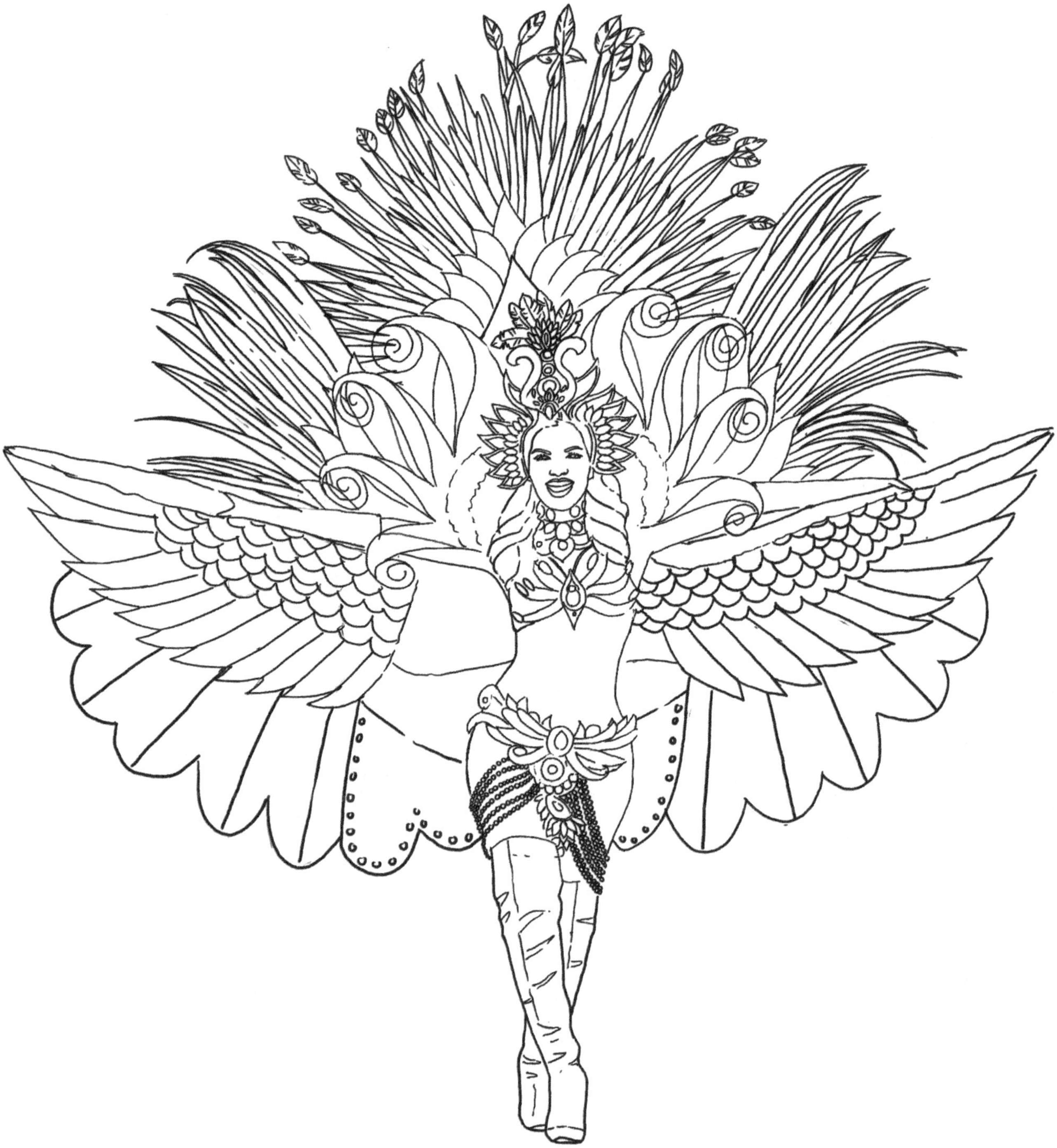

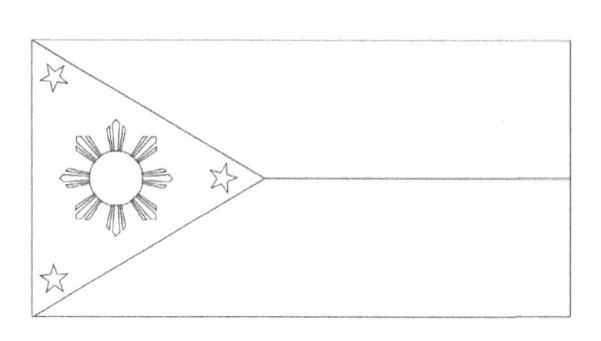

{ PHILIPPINES }

One-piece swimsuit, embellished boots and wings made of felt, rubber and fiber optic lights

INSPIRATION: Inspired by the ParuParo festival held in Dasmarinas, Cavite City in the Philippines every 26th of November which symbolizes the transformation of the city over the years. The festival depicts, in a parade of costumed street dancers, the metamorphosis of the butterfly much to what is happening in the city and in the Philippines.

STYLE: Modern take on Paruparo costumes as seen in the festivals

MATERIAL: Swarovski crystals, beaded one-piece swimsuit and wings are made of rubber and felt cloth

DESIGN: Executed in a one piece swimsuit and vibrant boots which is hand-embroidered and embellished with beads, swarovski crystals and sequins depicting the flamboyant

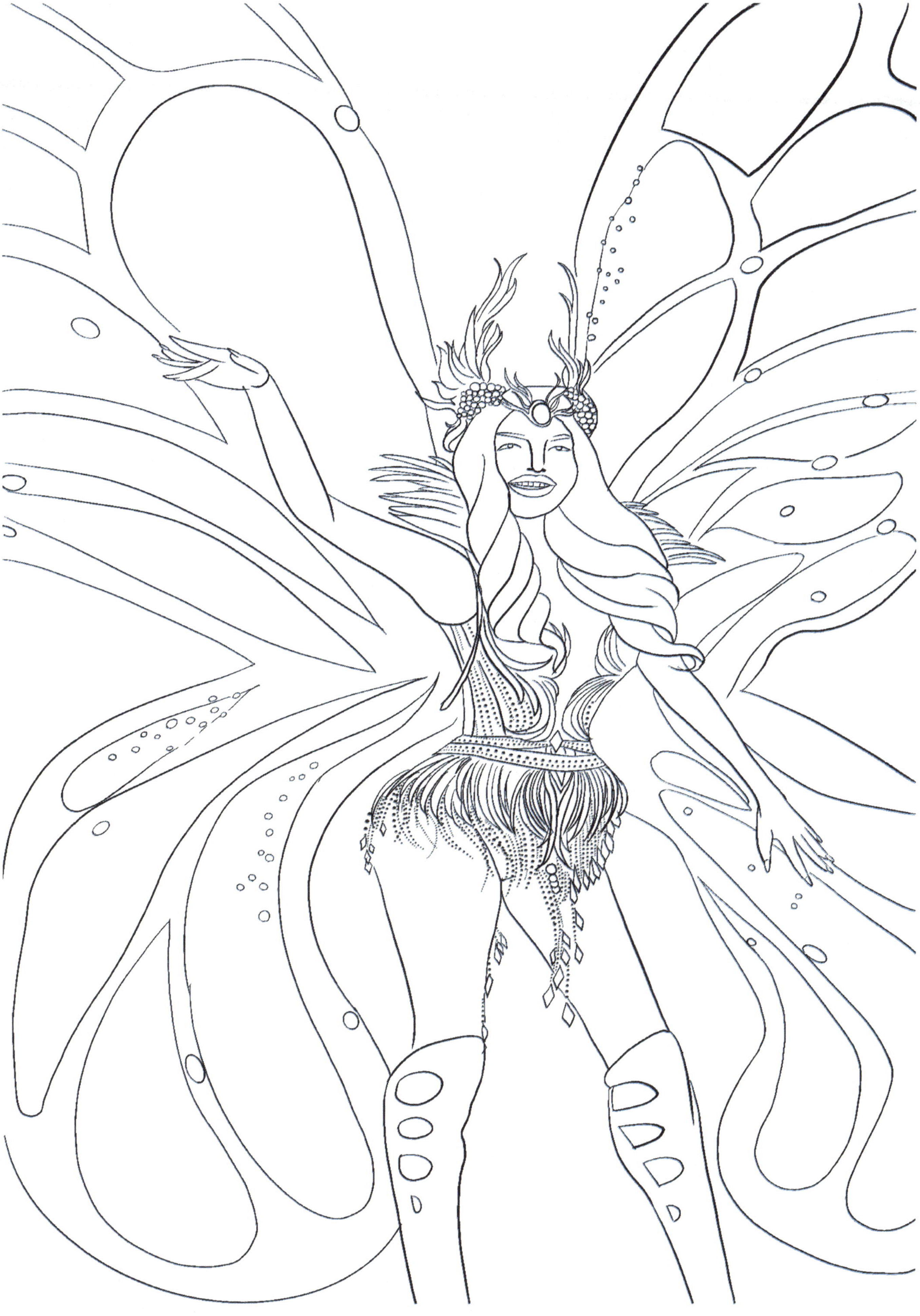

PORTUGAL

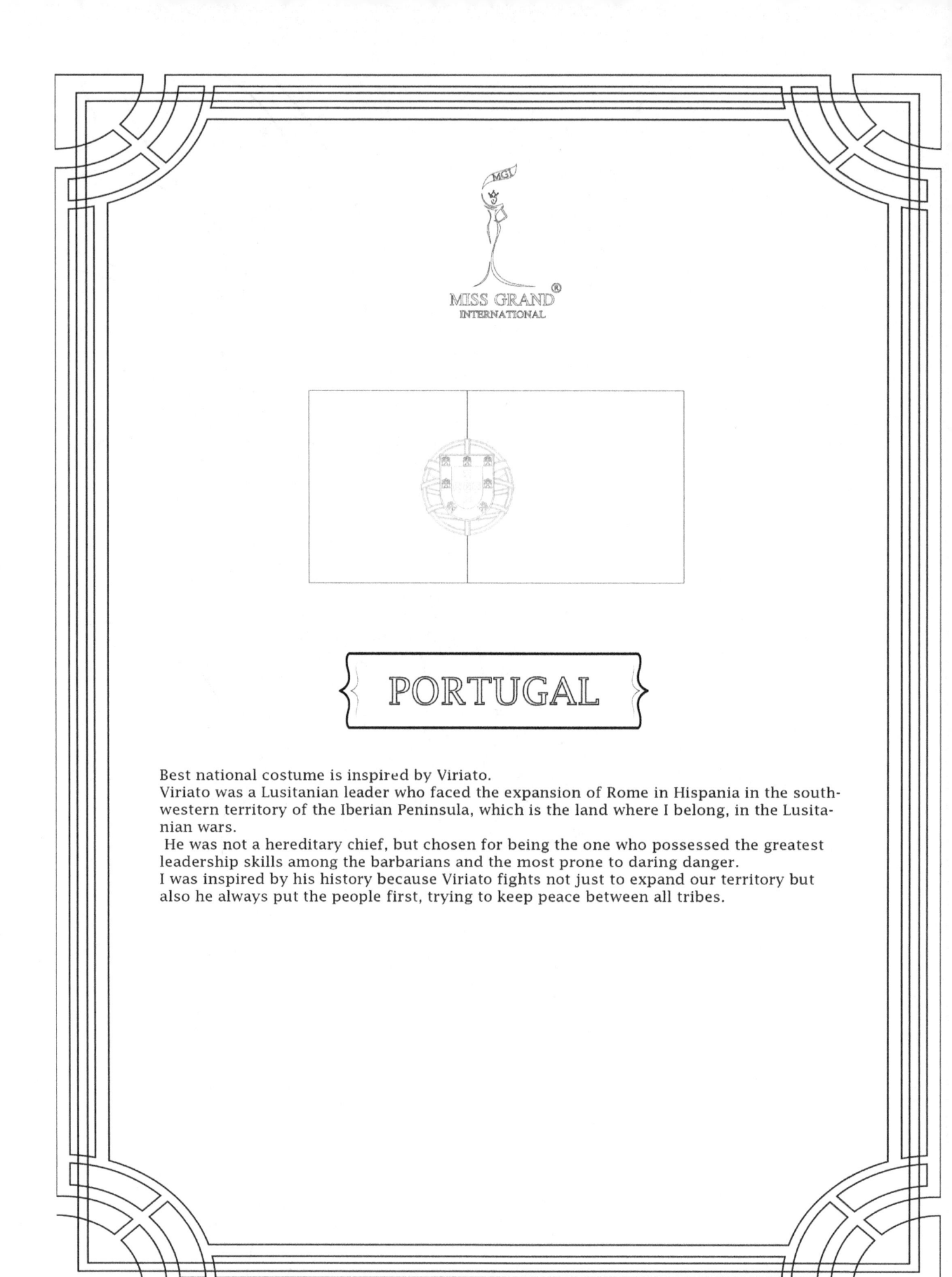

Best national costume is inspired by Viriato.
Viriato was a Lusitanian leader who faced the expansion of Rome in Hispania in the southwestern territory of the Iberian Peninsula, which is the land where I belong, in the Lusitanian wars.
 He was not a hereditary chief, but chosen for being the one who possessed the greatest leadership skills among the barbarians and the most prone to daring danger.
I was inspired by his history because Viriato fights not just to expand our territory but also he always put the people first, trying to keep peace between all tribes.

PUERTO RICO

Goddess Atabey is the supreme goddess of the Tainos, one of the two supreme deities in the Taino religion. She was worshipped as a goddess of fresh water and fertility; she is the female entity representing the Earth, the Spirit of the sun and the Spirit of all horizontal water, lakes, streams, the sea and sea tides. This deity was one of the most important for the native tribes that inhabited the Caribbean islands of the Antilles, mainly in Puerto Rico.

The dress was hand-woven, has 10 techniques of fabrics in "Macrame" It consists of 14 Carat gold sheets, Austrian crystals, swarovski and 2,500 meters of walnut thread. The confection lasted 6 months and has a weight of 39 kilograms. The colors represent the sea, the sun and the grandeur of Puerto Rican women

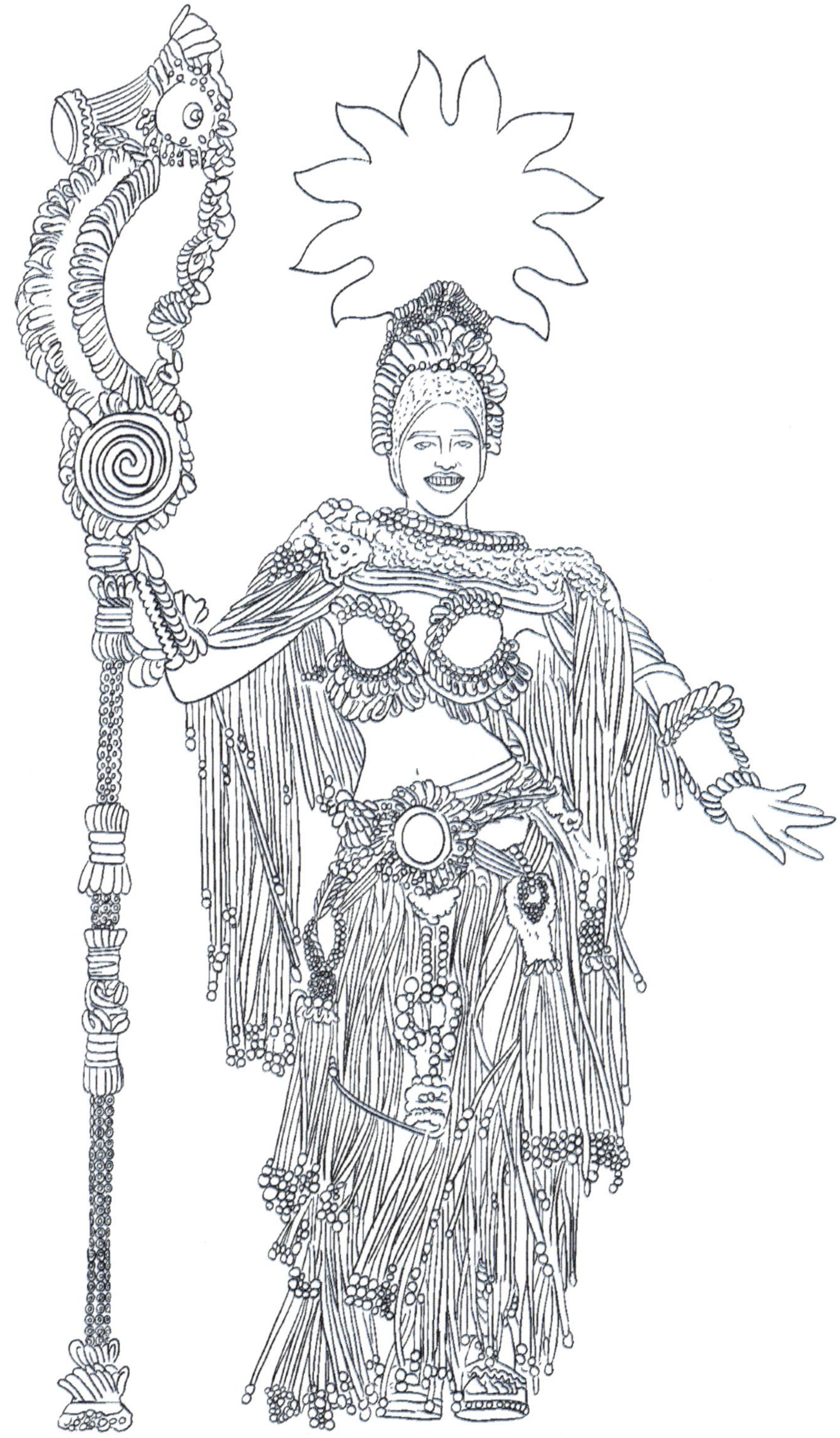

RUSSIA

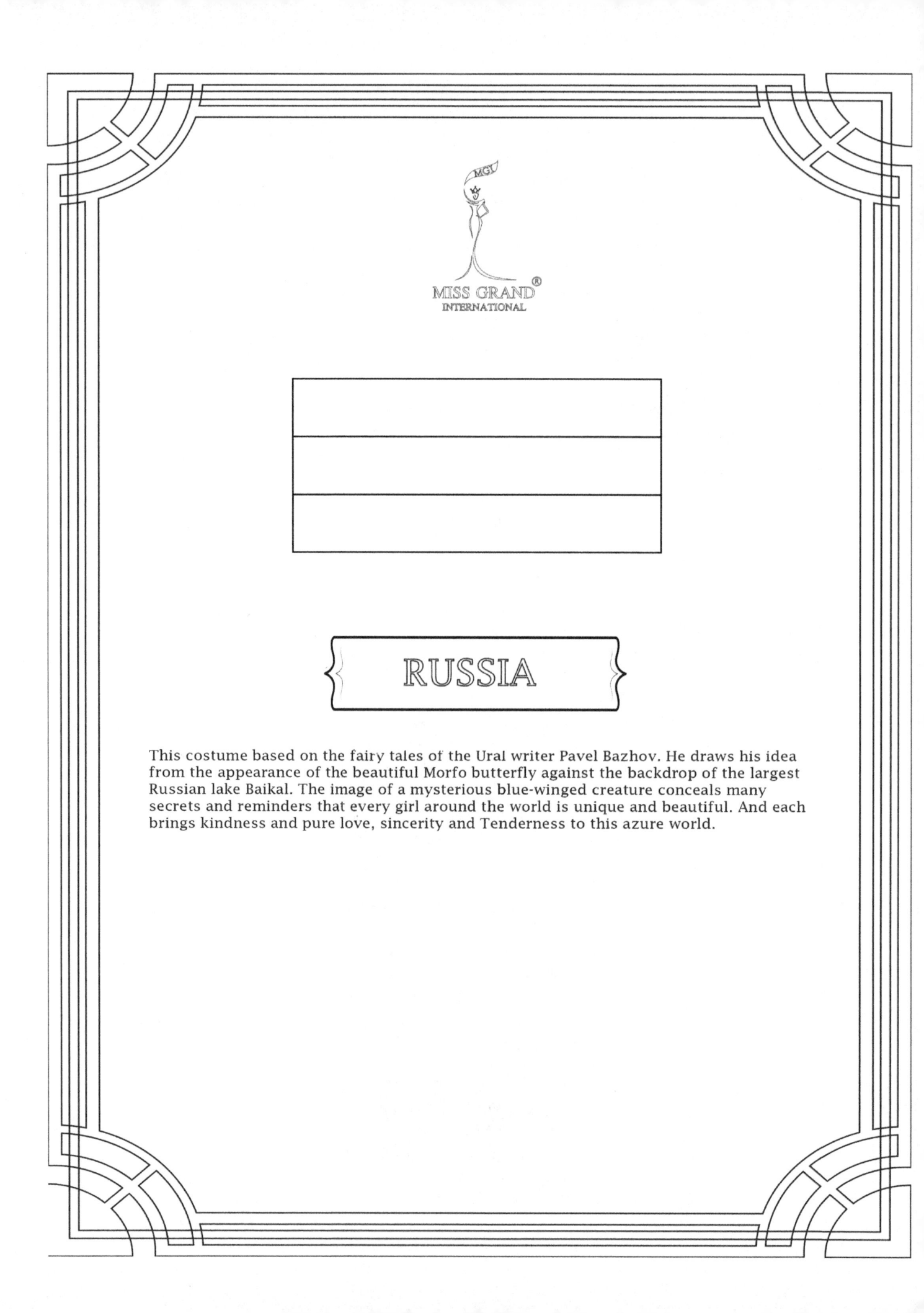

This costume based on the fairy tales of the Ural writer Pavel Bazhov. He draws his idea from the appearance of the beautiful Morfo butterfly against the backdrop of the largest Russian lake Baikal. The image of a mysterious blue-winged creature conceals many secrets and reminders that every girl around the world is unique and beautiful. And each brings kindness and pure love, sincerity and Tenderness to this azure world.

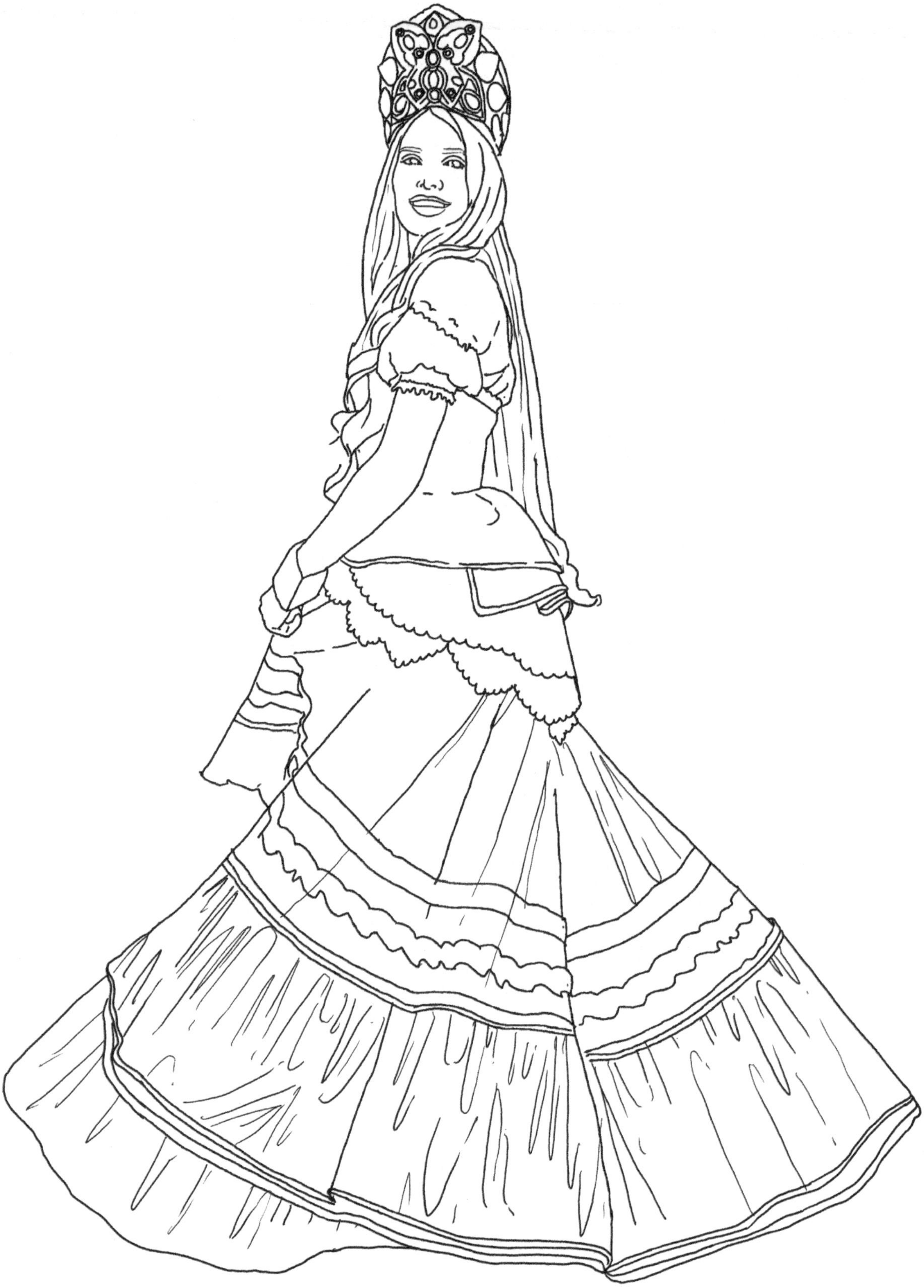

MISS GRAND INTERNATIONAL

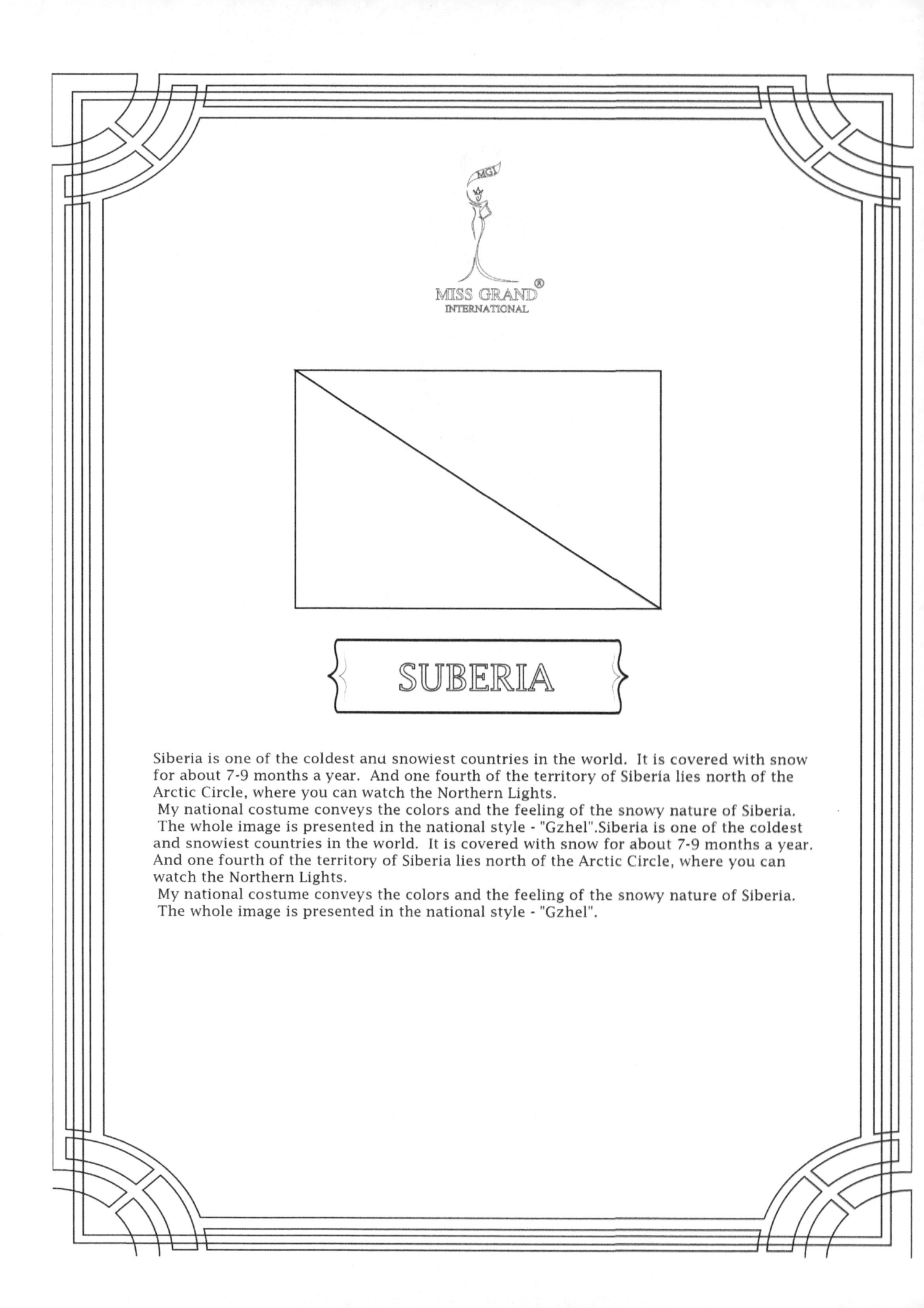

{ SUBERIA }

Siberia is one of the coldest and snowiest countries in the world. It is covered with snow for about 7-9 months a year. And one fourth of the territory of Siberia lies north of the Arctic Circle, where you can watch the Northern Lights.
 My national costume conveys the colors and the feeling of the snowy nature of Siberia. The whole image is presented in the national style - "Gzhel".Siberia is one of the coldest and snowiest countries in the world. It is covered with snow for about 7-9 months a year. And one fourth of the territory of Siberia lies north of the Arctic Circle, where you can watch the Northern Lights.
 My national costume conveys the colors and the feeling of the snowy nature of Siberia. The whole image is presented in the national style - "Gzhel".

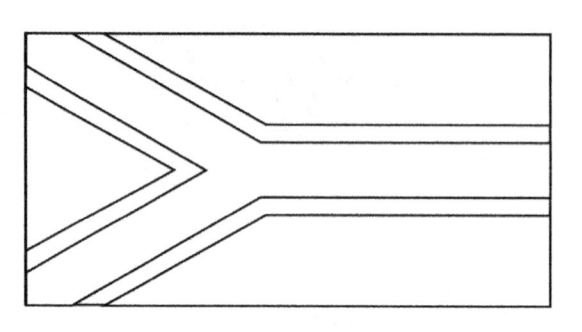

SOUTH AFRICA

Best National Costume was inspired by the wise words of one of our Late Legendary Leaders Mr Nelson Mandela "It always seems Impossible until it's done". Words that carried our great National Rugby Team "The Springboks" as they not only produced an inspiring performance but also brought hope to a country with complex history. My costume is a symbol of a multiracial, multicultural team working together to show that we are STRONGER TOGETHER. The Green symbolizes growth, renewal and rebirth and the gold symbolizes strength, and resilience which is what South Africa is.

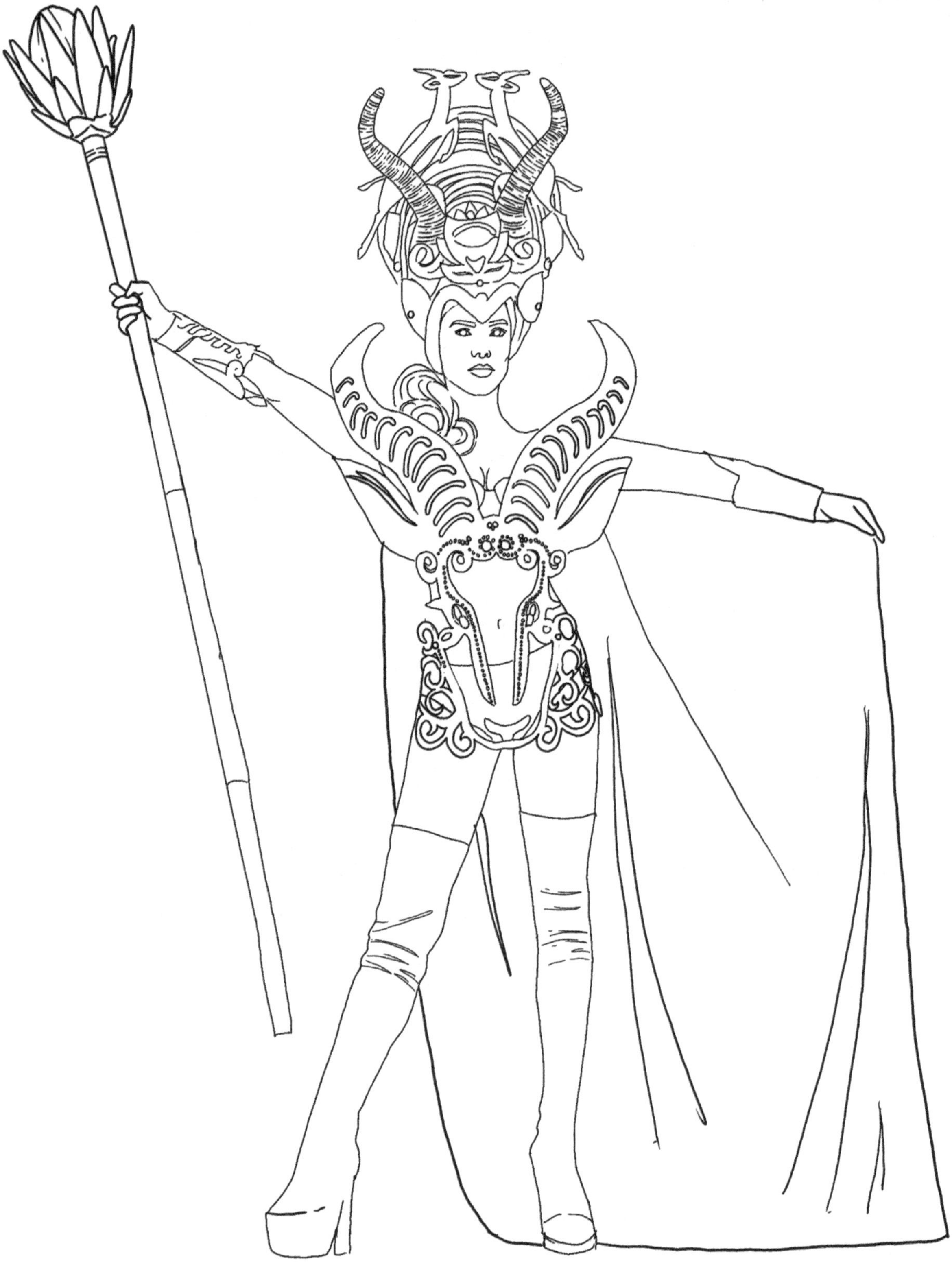

SPAIN

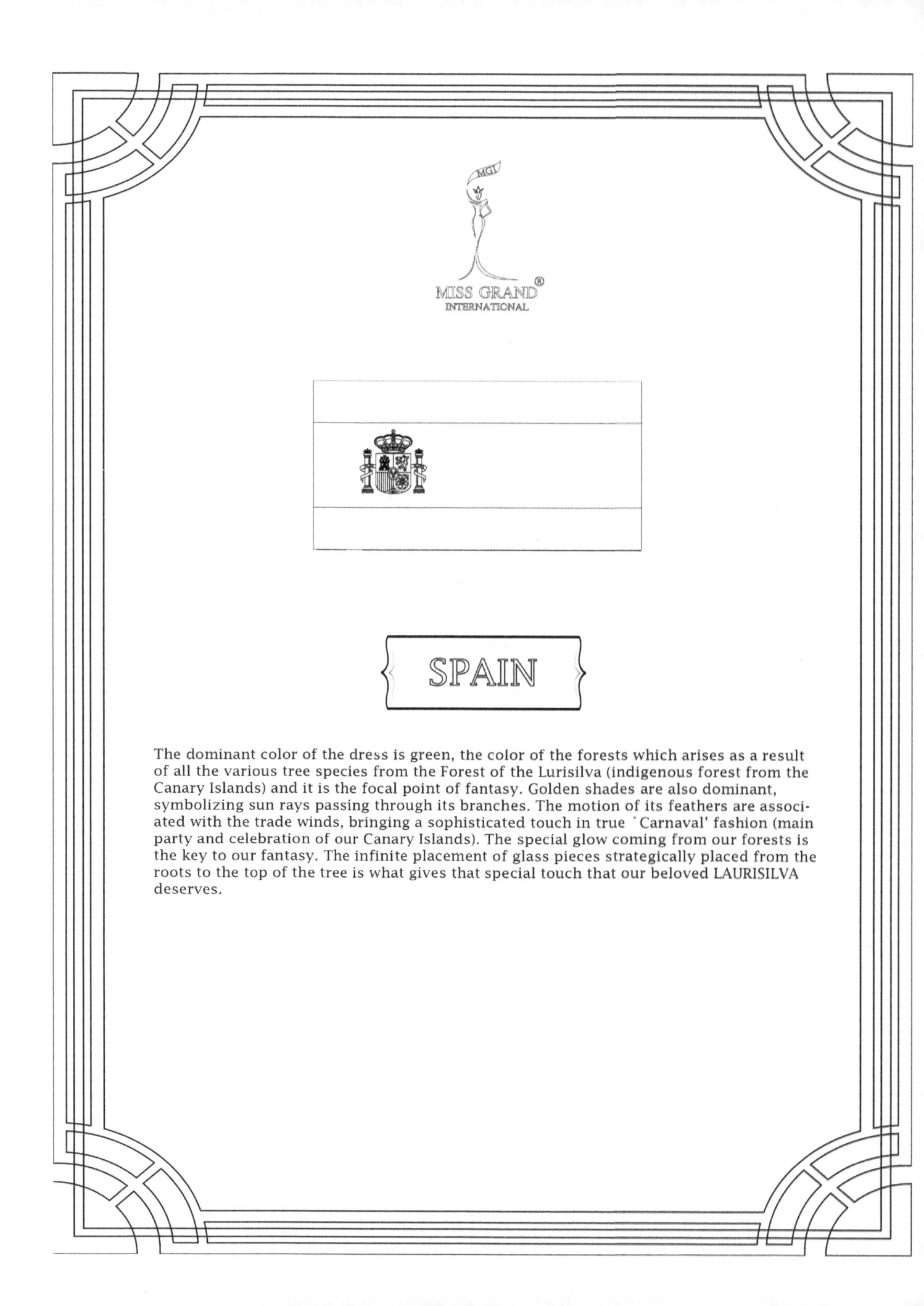

The dominant color of the dress is green, the color of the forests which arises as a result of all the various tree species from the Forest of the Lurisilva (indigenous forest from the Canary Islands) and it is the focal point of fantasy. Golden shades are also dominant, symbolizing sun rays passing through its branches. The motion of its feathers are associated with the trade winds, bringing a sophisticated touch in true 'Carnaval' fashion (main party and celebration of our Canary Islands). The special glow coming from our forests is the key to our fantasy. The infinite placement of glass pieces strategically placed from the roots to the top of the tree is what gives that special touch that our beloved LAURISILVA deserves.

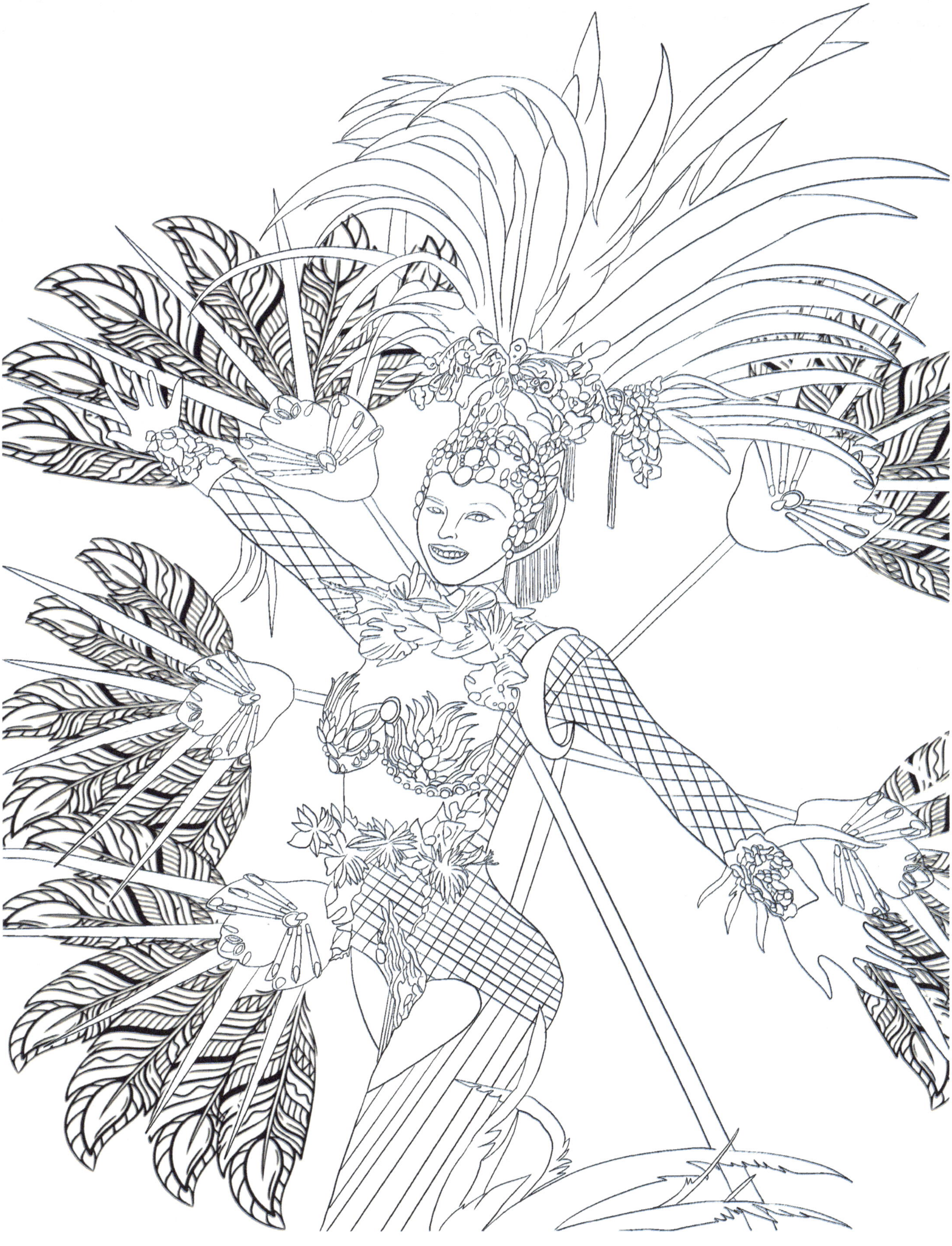

SRI LANKA

The concept of the kandy an saree is a modest but womanly piece of art. The Sinhalese culture values the kandyan saree, as the most elegant and versatile attire a woman can wear. The key feature of this saree is that the midriff is covered with a longer blouse, which is believed to make the garment more modest and protective against the heat. The kandyan saree is still worn by Sri Lankan brides, although a white wedding dress is another common outfit for reception ceremonies in this culture. The wedding saree, being of the utmost grace and elegant, is often made with finer materials like silk and decorated heavily with embroidery. The concept of the kandy an saree is a modest but womanly piece of art. The Sinhalese culture values the kandyan saree, as the most elegant and versatile attire a woman can wear. The key feature of this saree is that the midriff is covered with a longer blouse, which is believed to make the garment more modest and protective against the heat. The kandyan saree is still worn by Sri Lankan brides, although a white wedding dress is another common outfit for reception ceremonies in this culture. The wedding saree, being of the utmost grace and elegant, is often made with finer materials like silk and decorated heavily with embroidery.

SWEDEN

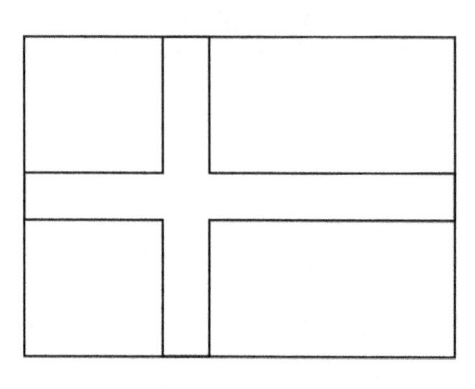

In sweden, december is the darkest and coldest season of the year. some days the sun does not rise at all. On December 13, Lucia is celebrated all around in Sweden. With light in her hair and with a singing choir, she comes with a hope for a brighter future. Lucia symbolizes love and joy. In television swedens lucia is appointed and each city also choose a lucia that will represent Lucia.

The costume is inspired by sweden's cold days with snow but under the cold hides a beautiful lucia with light in her hair. Here she comes walking with the hope of a brighter future and love.

(The long beautiful dressjacket symbolizes the cold snow, under the jacket a beautiful dress is hidden that will be come front and symbolize the wonderful Lucia that brings light and love to us.)

THAILAND

Inspired by the Ramayana literature, the episode "Hanuman Lifting the Heart Box" telling the story of the giant Tosakan as he was angry with Hanuman, the ape who could steal his heart box.

Presented in the form of the contemporary Thai masked dance drama or Khon which is ornately decorated with crystals conveying the strength of the giant through the wearer. The national costume is applied to the puppetry of Hanuman in the pose of "Khuen Loy Khon", which is one of the battle stances of the elegant high-class dances. It is considered an invaluable cultural heritage of Thailand.

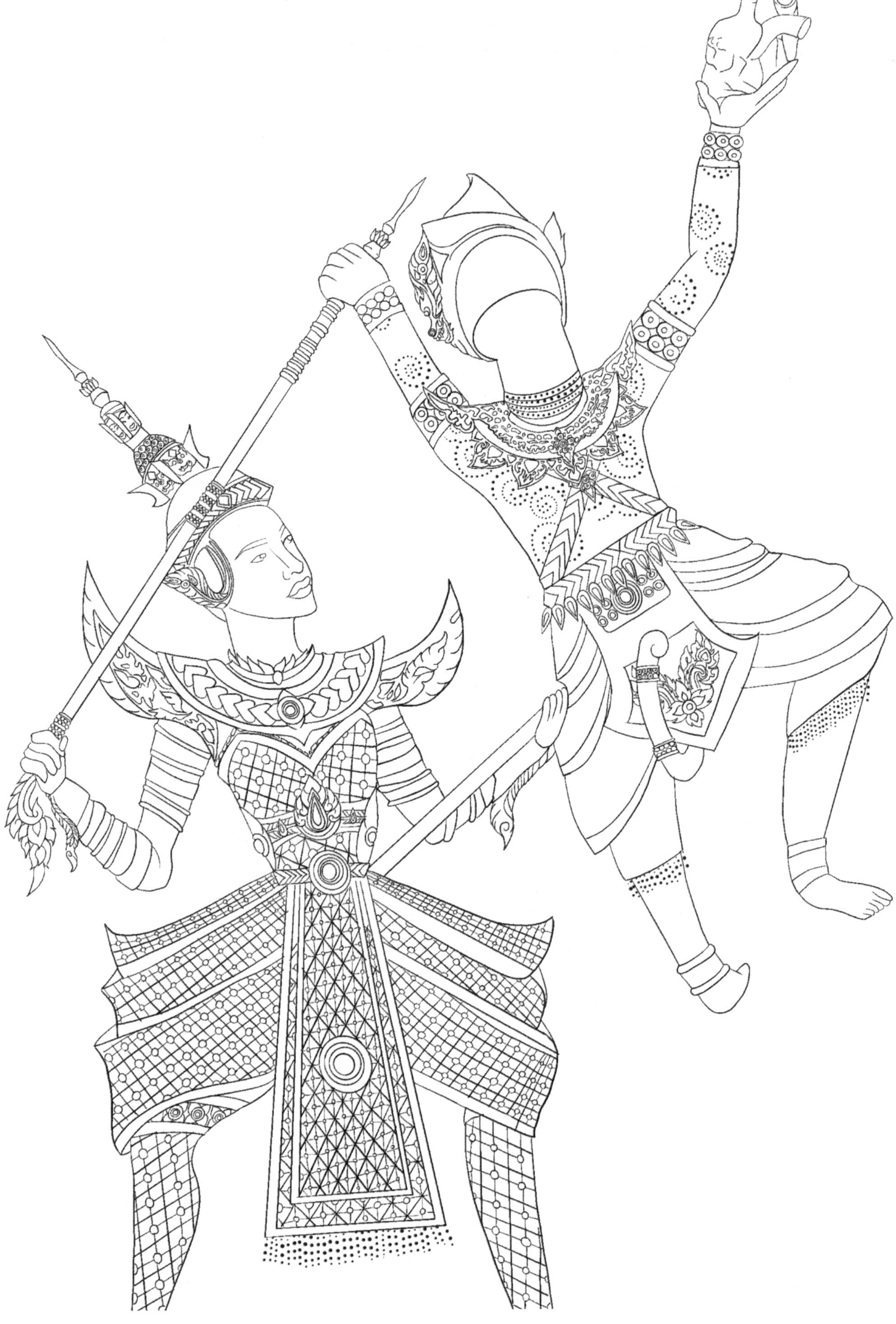

UNITED STATES OF AMERICA

Breast Cancer Awarness - My meaning behind raising awarness for breast cancer is because being a women and having the amazing platform of Miss Grand United States, I think I'd be doing a huge disservice to women across the world if I didnt speak out for women who are currently fighting or have fought for their lives against Breast cancer. Over 2.3 million women are affected in the United States, about 43,600 women will die from breast cancer. On Average every 2 mintues a women is diagnosed with breast cancer in the United States.

Women are the creators of life, we most do our part to protect, support and lift up every women. This costume stands for all the stong women acorss the globe fighting cancer. We must support the fighters, admire the surviors, remember the angels and never give up hope. Together we are tougher than cancer.

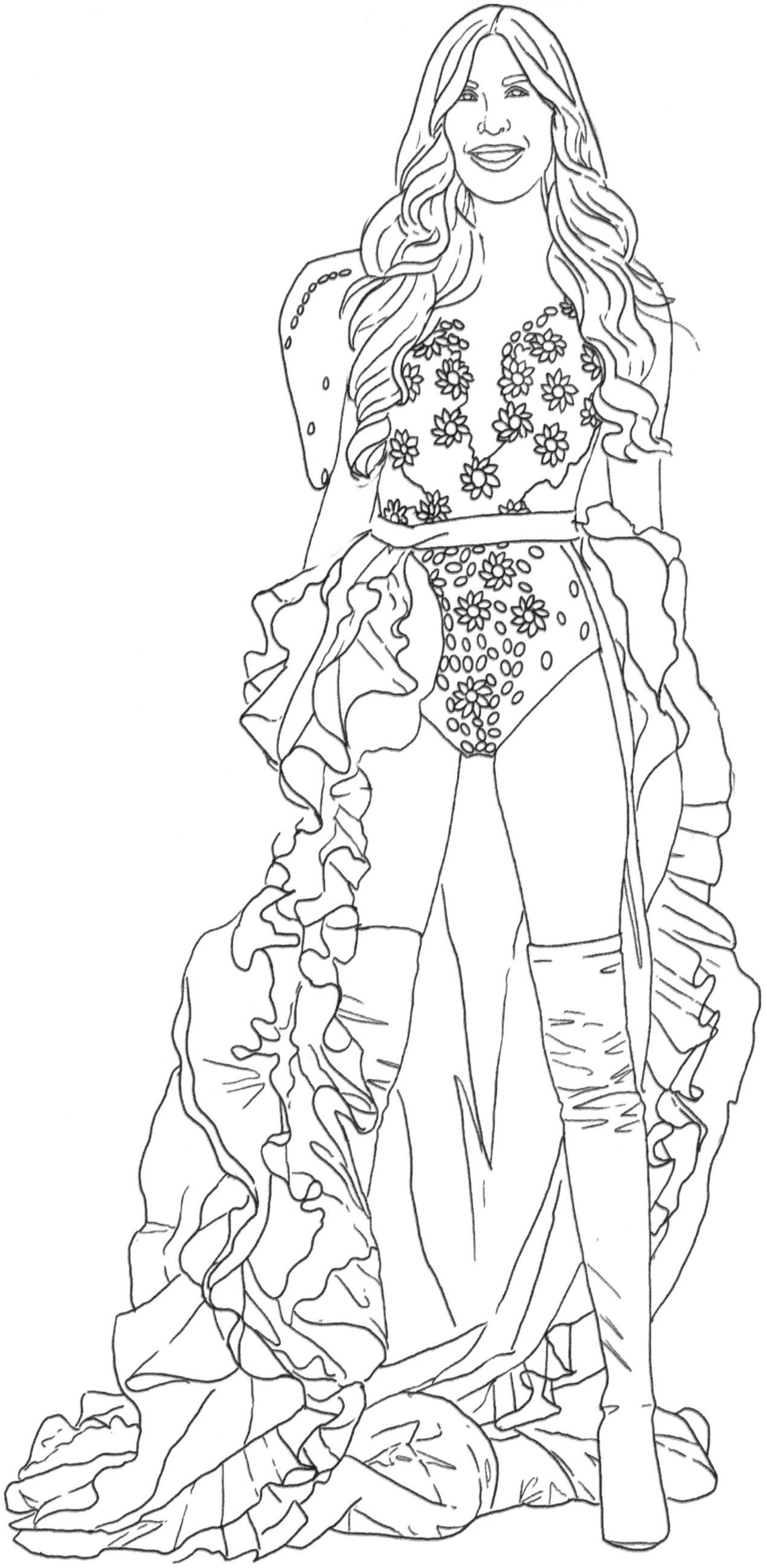

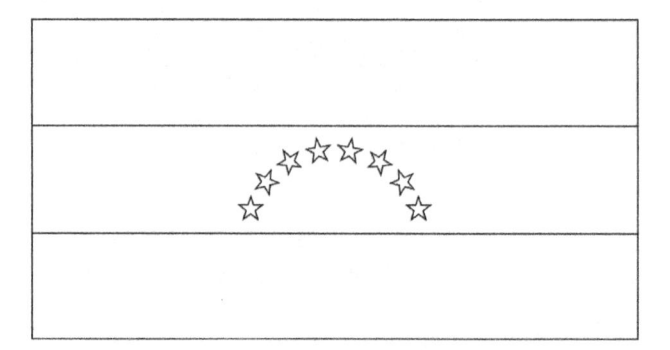

VENEZUELA

Following the majesty, the mysticism of our myths and legends, this time the story of the Ipure snake made woman resurfaces, an origin that is remote from the CAPAYACUAR indigenous population in the Monagas state, a place where charms happen and of which it is native. Vanessa Coello, Miss Grand International 2021 ... divinity and beauty emerges from the waters of the Ipure River, the rebirth of the innocence, purity and beauty of the female gender with the strength of the serpent, in a wonderful fantasy full of magical realism which represents "Deidad Capayacuar" a creation of the famous Valencian designer Carlos Pérez, in which inspired by one of the best-known stories of the Monagas state, the beautiful Vanessa Cohelo represents the transition of the Ipure snake, in a work completely by hand embroidery, scales covered with hundreds of degrading crystals on the middle of its body, at the other end the ecdysis can be seen What happens in the snakes, showing the innocence and purity represented by that girl from the Capayacuar tribes, protagonist of the story in a work of embroidery in crystals representing the femininity and beauty that the national orchid possesses in lilac colors

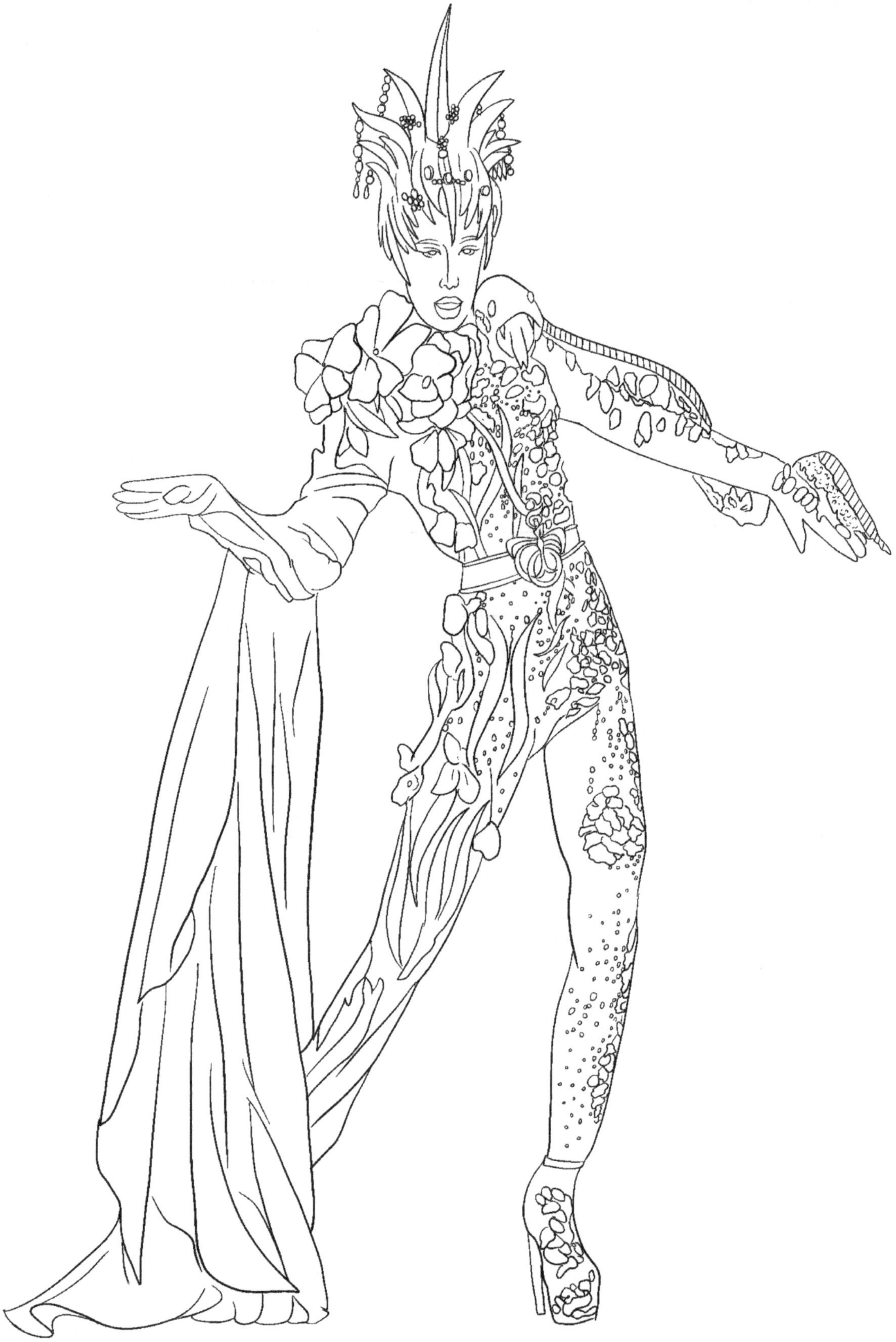

VIETNAM

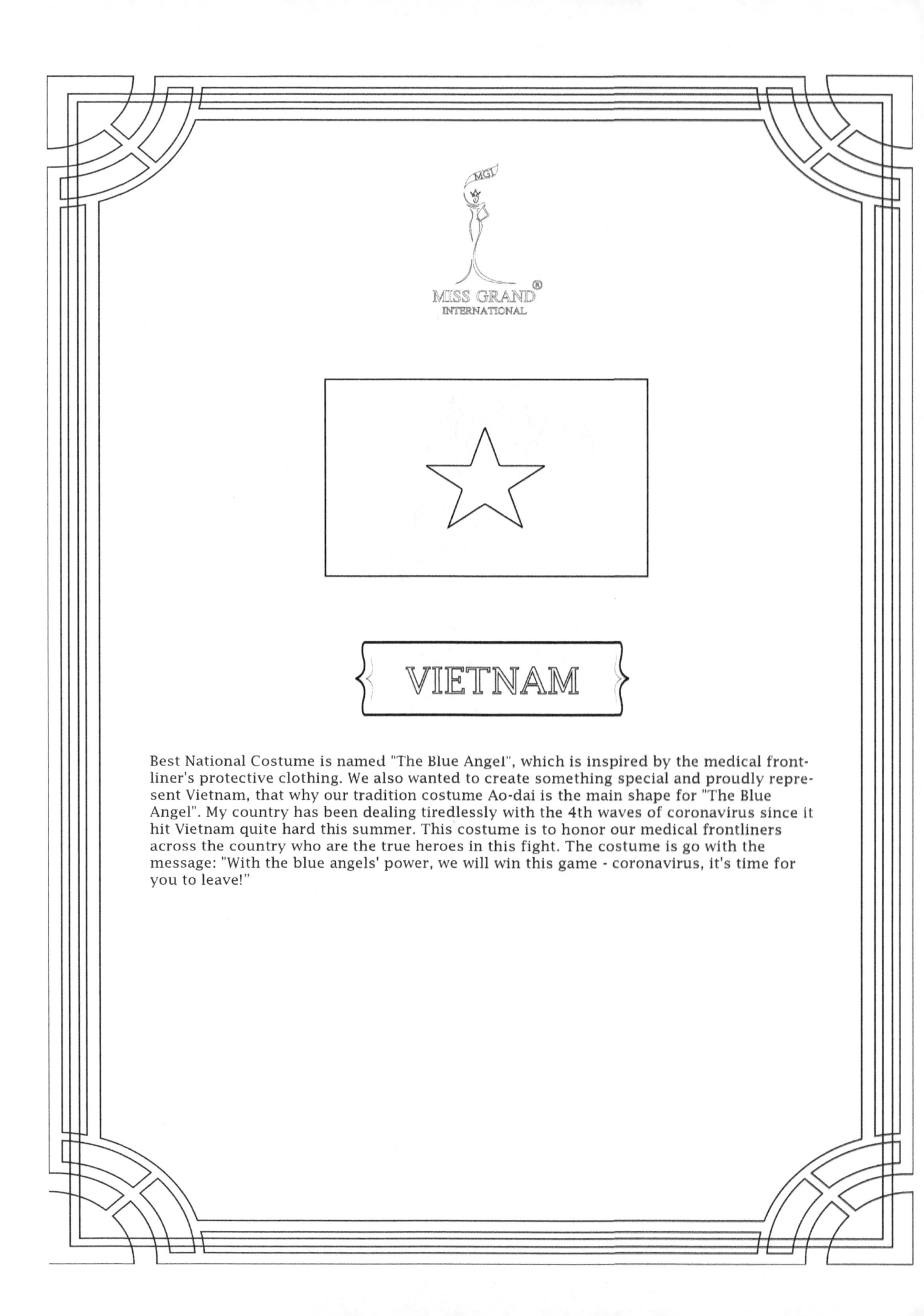

Best National Costume is named "The Blue Angel", which is inspired by the medical frontliner's protective clothing. We also wanted to create something special and proudly represent Vietnam, that why our tradition costume Ao-dai is the main shape for "The Blue Angel". My country has been dealing tiredlessly with the 4th waves of coronavirus since it hit Vietnam quite hard this summer. This costume is to honor our medical frontliners across the country who are the true heroes in this fight. The costume is go with the message: "With the blue angels' power, we will win this game - coronavirus, it's time for you to leave!"

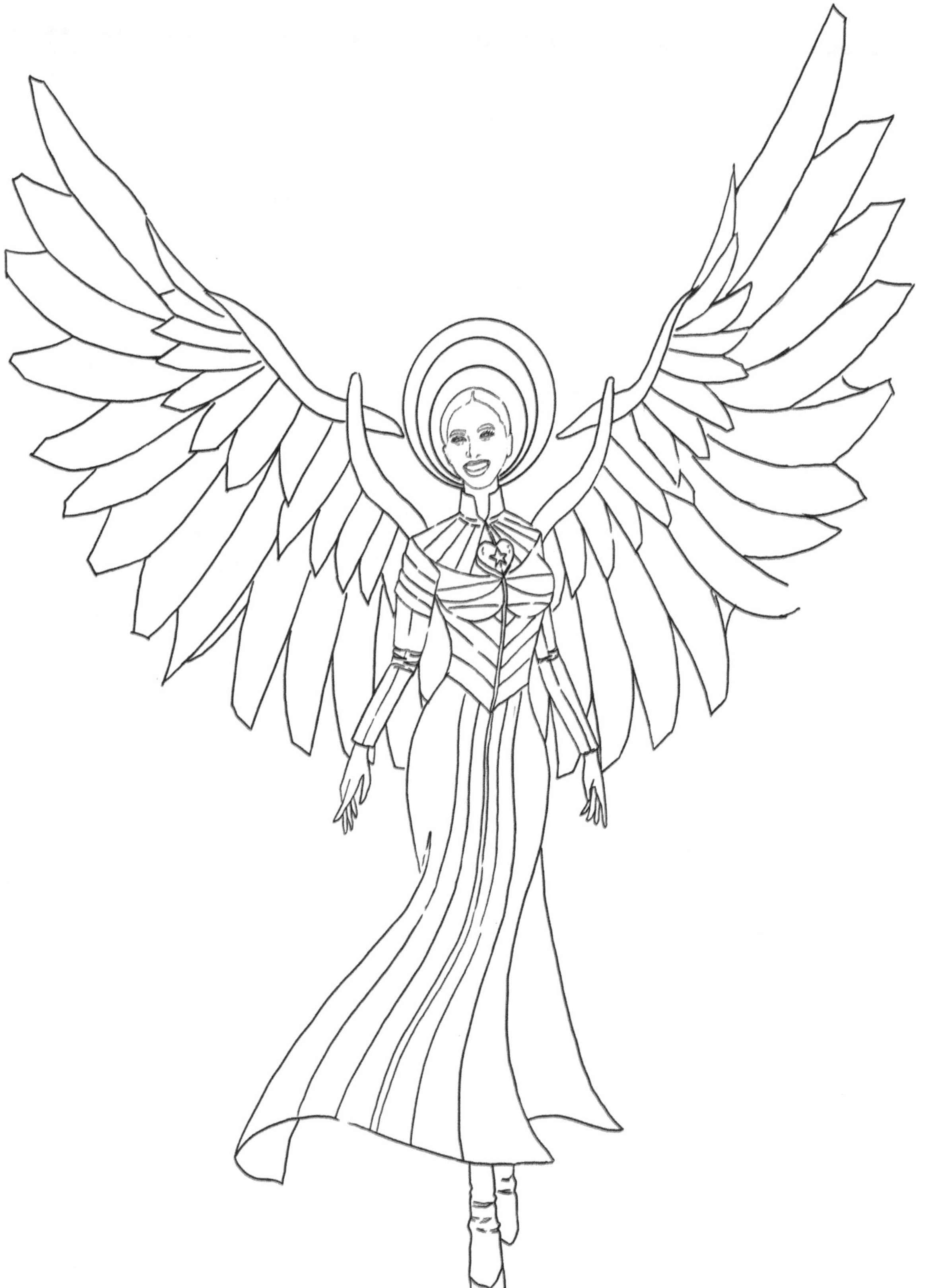

MISS GRAND
INTERNATIONAL

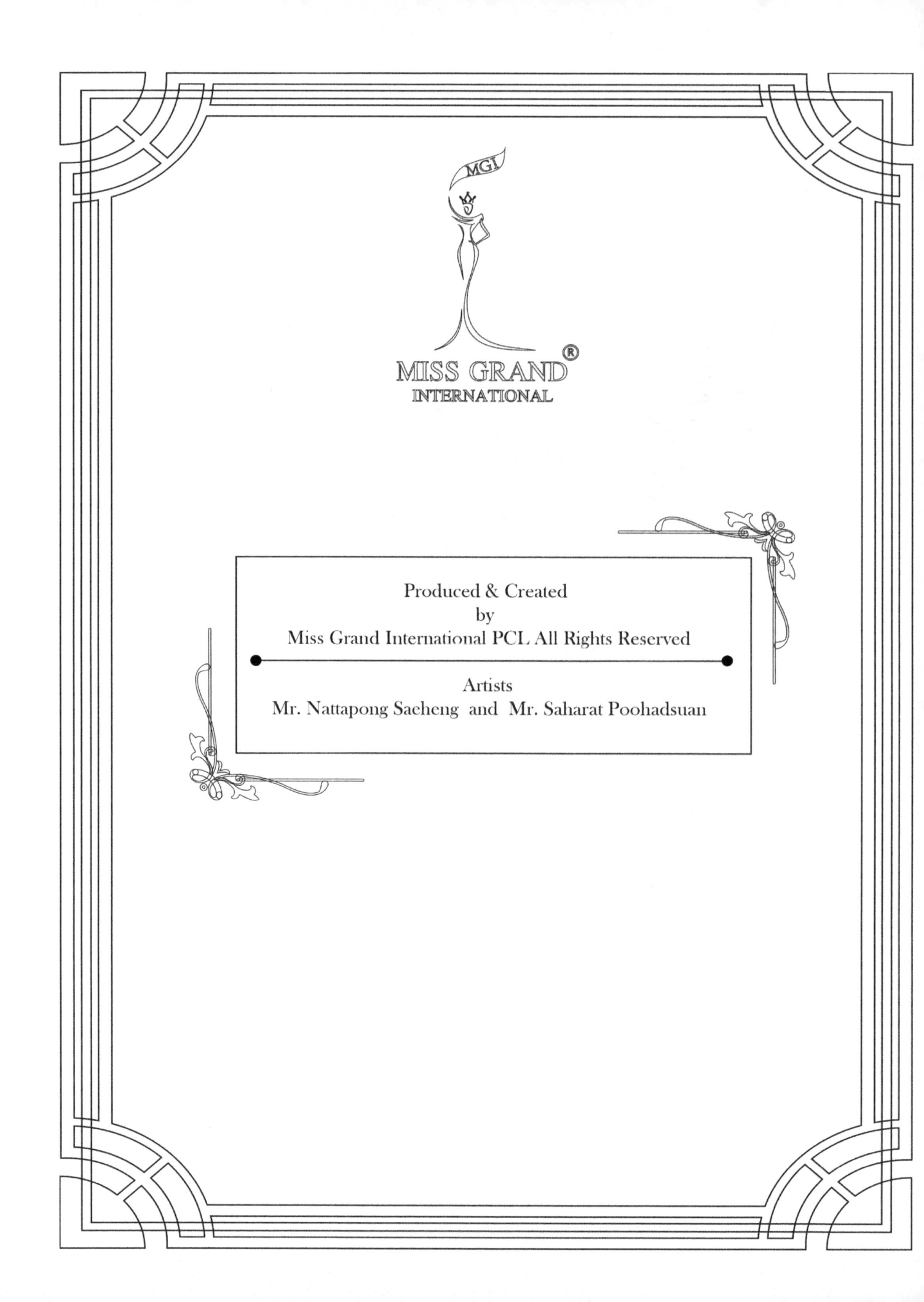

Produced & Created
by
Miss Grand International PCL All Rights Reserved

Artists
Mr. Nattapong Saeheng and Mr. Saharat Poohadsuan

Made in the USA
Las Vegas, NV
13 April 2025